Worldly Spirituality

Worldly Spirituality

Biblical Reflections on Money, Politics, and Sex

William Robert McClelland

CBP Press
St. Louis, Missouri

Scripture quotations, unless otherwise indicated, are from the Revised Standard Version of the Bible, copyrighted 1946, 1952, © 1971, 1973, by the Division of Christian Education of the National Council of Churches in the United States of America and are used by permission. In some instances, references may be paraphrased for inclusiveness or clarity.

Scriptures marked NEB are from *The New English Bible*, © 1976. The Delegates of the Oxford University Press, Inc., and The Syndics of the Cambridge University Press, 1961, 1970. Reprinted by permission.

Library of Congress Cataloging-in-Publication Data

McClelland, W. Robert (William Robert), 1931-
    Worldly spirituality / W. Robert McClelland.
160 p.   cm.
    Includes bibliographical references.
    ISBN 0-8272-4227-1 : $10.95
    1. Wealth—Religious aspects—Christianity.   2. Christianity and
politics.   3. Sex—Religious aspects—Christianity.   4. Spiritual life—
Presbyterian authors.   I. Title.
BR115.W4M33   1990
241—dc20   89-27538
                                                                           CIP

Printed in the United States of America

To Bonnie L. Montle
for all the years of help and encouragement

Acknowledgments

This work has taken shape across the years as I gathered together into one place ideas that have themselves been developing over a long period of time. The lines of indebtedness, therefore, range far beyond the simple preparation of a manuscript. Yet for that help in preparing the finished work, I am truly grateful: to Dr. David Peterson and Judith Smith for exegetical input, the Rev. William Gay for reading the manuscript and offering critical suggestions, Bonnie Montle for hours spent at the typewriter, and Herb Lambert for overseeing the process of producing a finished book.

Reaching further back, I recall with pleasant memories and deep gratitude the hospitality of Betsy and David Peterson when some of this material was presented in a summer school for pastors at Iliff School of Theology. To members of the Illinois Association of Campus Pastors, who heard and refined other ideas, as well as individual members of numerous churches where, through classes and retreats, thoughts were honed on the grindstone of public discussion—appreciation. I remember, too, my faculty colleagues at Illinois College, where these thoughts survived the honest questioning of those searching for truth. They kept my feet on the ground while I tried to find the functional equivalents necessary to make sense of the faith in an agnostic setting. Lastly, I would be remiss if I did not acknowledge the life and generosity of George Foster, whose financial assistance made possible a sabbatical year of study at the University of Edinburgh, where the original research and reflection was begun. To all, I am indebted and deeply grateful.

W. Robert McClelland
St. Louis, 1990

Contents

Introduction

The emotional reaction of many Christians to Martin Scorsese's film *The Last Temptation of Christ* demonstrated how some believers feel, not only about Christ's interest in sex, but about other aspects of life as well. Such areas of life as making money or involvement in politics have been denied spiritual guidance and counsel because they are believed to be, if not ungodly, at least too worldly for the serious Christian's consideration.

While it may be true that professional theologians are now grappling with these concerns, it is also true that their conversations have largely been carried on among themselves and not with the church at large. The result has been that their words of wisdom have gone unnoticed by rank and file believers in the pew or—in the case of Scorsese's film—in the street. Attempts at public dialogue, not only in theaters, but in public schools, and certainly in the church, have been opposed by well meaning but, at least as far as the professional theological discussion is concerned, unenlightened Christians.

When Robin Roberts received one of the many awards in his long and colorful baseball career, he received it with proper modesty and words to the effect that his real ambition was to get to heaven, where the really significant awards would be given. His humble acceptance speech illustrates a widespread assumption held by many religious people: The purpose of life is to get to heaven, and spirituality is meant to provide the means and the discipline for doing so.

Heaven is where the real action is. Everything else is secondary and preliminary. Not only does this world with all of its concerns pale into insignificance in light of the greater value of heaven, but life here is seen as merely preparation for the next. What we do here in this world, with this life, is only significant in light of its meaning for the other world, beyond death. The kingdom of God is understood as otherworldly and, in popular consciousness, comes to be synonymous with the "kingdom of heaven." Consequently, worldly interests are of no great concern to pilgrim believers, who strive to remain untarnished by them. Godly concerns are not found here, but in the yet-to-come kingdom of heaven. Spirituality concerns itself with "disciplines of the

Spirit," such things as ways to read the Bible, methods of praying, the value of fasting, and the importance of self-denial.

Christian thought took this otherworldly turn early in its development. The theology of the early church assumed the world was bound for hell on a fast express. There was nothing good to be said about it in its present condition, and there was no reason to redeem it. People, yes! They could be saved—or at least their immortal souls could be salvaged. But their bodies, worldly goods, and everything else on the face of the earth was, in the end, doomed to destruction under the wrath of God. The good news, as Christian spirituality has interpreted it, is that God has prepared a safe haven away from the corruption of this world where perfection awaits believers. God forgives sins and asks us to live virtuous lives untainted by worldly infections so that we can pass inspection at the pearly gates.

A Martin Luther King Jr. would have been as alien in the early church as a Martian because his concern, and that of other social reformers, was to save the world by changing its institutions and social structures. Social reform assumes that the world has value. It requires getting the hands dirty. But if worldly concerns are by nature sinful and have no value in the divine scheme of things, then there is little point in giving them serious consideration as matters of spiritual importance. Quite logically, therefore, the apostle Paul admonished slaves to be good slaves, rather than unite to strike or overthrow the oppressive establishment. His spirituality exhorted believers to exhibit the kind of virtues that would be pleasing to God and appropriate for heaven, such as honesty, patience, and hard work.

But today we feel more at home in the world than did our faith ancestors. We look at the world as a source of personal fulfillment through work, family ties, and governmental services. Heaven may be our home, but we are not homesick.

What is needed, therefore, is a spirituality for living in this world. Christian spirituality must come down to earth. It needs to help us change our attitudes about the world and provide us with ethical guidance for involvement in its affairs. New thought is required to put the practicalities of our daily life in touch with our faith.

Unfortunately, we are hobbled by this lingering belief that God is interested in religion but not in life, in what goes on in church but not in the bedroom, the boardroom, or the oval office. For example, when the minister came to dinner in my childhood home, the conversation was usually kept safe by talking about religion or the weather. Certainly not controversial topics and, most assuredly, not money, sex, or politics. Yet these topics are very much part of worldly conversation. Because they are worldly concerns, they have been regarded as taboo topics by the church. Discussion of them has been moralistic, guarded, or denied. As Christians we are not accustomed to revealing our incomes to one another. We hide them from view just as we do our sexuality, even as we keep our political views to ourselves. We feel they are of no concern to anyone but ourselves or our most intimate loved ones, and certainly no concern of the church.

In actuality this kind of spirituality ignores the experience of God. It overlooks the Old Testament's beginning with a creation story that moves the focus of faith from heaven to earth and the New Testament's concluding vision of a new creation involving a better world. The divine Word becomes flesh in a barn, and the throne of grace is not a pontifical chair high above the crowds, but a cross socketed in the earth between two thieves. Faith puts the focus on the world, and there is where it must always look to avoid a false spirituality. Biblical spirituality calls us to seek after true worldliness—in the sense of a more godly interpretation of business, ballot, and bedroom, where so much of our energy, thought, and time are spent.

By focusing on the biblical view of Christ and creation, we will see the fundamental flaw in traditional religious attitudes toward money, politics, and sex. We will see that a worldly spirituality calls us to share our wealth, our political views, and our love with others as a matter of holy calling in order to continue God's creative initiative. We will regard the Bible as a worldly book of wisdom, and on the topics of money, politics, and sex—about which the church has been so silent or negative—we will see that it has a great deal to say positively. It sets forth its views in story form, and it is to these stories that we turn in the pages that follow as we explore these worldly goods.

Chapter One

Making Money Is Not a Sin

Living seems to require that we die and pay taxes—or so it is often said. If so, we must admit that while traditional spirituality has aided us in our dying, it has offered little or no guidance in paying our taxes. Jesus' admonition "Render to Caesar the things that are Caesar's, and to God the things that are God's" (Mark 12:17) has been interpreted as a call to separate things godly and things worldly, as if the two were distinctly different and could be isolated from one another, thereby settling the matter.

In fact, the two cannot be so neatly compartmentalized. Paying taxes to Caesar involves the believer in the politics that levies and spends taxes in addition to earning the income on which the taxes are paid. Because money has power, it can help or hinder people along the path of their life's journey. How wealth is distributed is not only a political decision to be made, but a spiritual concern to people of faith. Money and politics, thereby, inevitably become "things" to be rendered to God. The believer's faith cannot be left out of any consideration of either.

For now, let us postpone the discussion of a political spirituality so that we may turn immediately to the matter of money. The spiritual issue concerning money has to do with our attitude about it and what we do with it.

I write as a Christian who remembers growing up in a home where religious discourse was common table conversation. Money, however, was never discussed and the family income was a taboo topic. I quickly learned that in polite company money was something one never talked about. Certainly a person's salary was as intimate a topic as sex and just as forbidden.

With maturity has come the sad realization that, in the eyes of the church at least, making money is not an honorable calling. Indeed, the church has looked with jaundiced eye upon not only "filthy lucre," but those who dirty their hands and compromise their souls by making it. The church has frequently warned its constituency, "Money is the root of all evil." That is a misquotation, of course. The correct one, from the apostle Paul's warning to his young protégé, Timothy, reads, "The love of money is the root of all evils" (1 Timothy 6:10). Nevertheless, religious people have taken the former quote to heart with the result that, as a group, professional church leaders are often poorly paid and poorly regarded by society, parishioners, and themselves.

I write, therefore, not only as a believer, but also as a minister of the gospel who has experienced the effects of this misguided teaching. Let me share personally as a member of the clergy profession. Vocational studies suggest that we choose to enter the ministry because we have not only a sense of divine calling, or a desire to serve God and humanity, but also a need for security. The regular paycheck and ready-made relationships of a warm womblike social group—both of which are offered by the church—meet this need. Psychological profiles indicate that we also have an inordinate need to be liked and appreciated by others. Frequently we regard ourselves as second-class citizens and exhibit low professional self-esteem. Sometimes we overcompensate for this by trying to prove to ourselves and others how much we are one of the gang. The end result of our insecurity and the need to be liked is a tendency to shortchange anything that resembles "prophetic" ministry. We are afraid to offend parishioners by our preaching and reluctant to bite the hand that feeds us with leadership that rocks the ecclesiastical boat.

We are caught between our emotional needs and the demands of the gospel. Because we know the Old Testament typically regarded prophets who were on the king's payroll as false prophets and their message as suspect, we feel we have compromised our integrity and our ministry.

Wealth could be a saving grace. Financial independence could free us for doing prophetic ministry just as it did for the prophet Amos. Recent biblical studies reveal that Amos was a relatively well-off member of the Judahite gentry. He was a landed member of his community involved in several types of agriculture. The prophet's use of very sophisticated language and his style of writing suggest considerable education. Because of his personal financial situation he was able to travel to the Northern Kingdom (Israel) and articulate a vigorous prophetic message that cut the establishment's conscience to the quick. Perhaps if we clergy were more financially independent—that is, less dependent on the institution for our support——we might be willing to risk a more prophetic ministry. If so, the church would benefit in the long run and God would be glorified.

Many times I have seen colleagues go to seed in a parish where they felt trapped. Frustrated because they wanted to move on to a fresh challenge, they could not find one that met their financial needs.

Staying where they were was not an option because ends did not meet on their present salary, so they dropped out of the ministry altogether, disillusioned.

Others felt they could not afford to leave, so they stayed, much to the detriment of themselves, the parish, and the church. To create a "tent ministry" was not even considered as a possibility. When ministers feel like prisoners sentenced to life in jail, something in them dies. Again, the end result is the loss of potentially good leadership to the church.

Instead of trying to convince ourselves and others that the Spirit always calls us to a "field of larger service," where the salary just happens to be larger, financial independence could free us to consider the calling of God on its own merits rather than on its economic benefits. Moreover, financial independence might free us to live and laugh at the awkward attempts of church and society to tame the fire within and manipulate us by pulling on our purse strings as if we were marionettes on stage to dance for their comfort and pleasure. If you are a clergy person and have never felt these tugs, you are a fortunate person, indeed, and a minority among your peers. That, or perhaps you have never risked enough to challenge the powers and principalities.

In any case, I have found that being financially independent as a clergy person has encouraged risky ministry and, in addition, has enhanced my self-esteem. Moreover, it has provided God with some additional money that I did not need to live on, with the result that some things have been achieved and some folks have been aided that would not otherwise have been the case.

The late Joseph Campbell observed that all money is congealed energy. Money, like the Spirit, can energize. It has power—power to do things that the Holy One cannot, or will not, do without it.

How many times have Christian pastors been in situations where, after all the words of love and the prayers of comfort have been offered, the really grace-full thing to do would have been to write out a check to meet the need? I am not suggesting for one minute that money can solve all human problems or that the words of love and the prayers of comfort are not important, only that money can do some things that nothing else can, and we need not only recognize this fact, but as emissaries of God's grace, equip ourselves with the financial resources for seizing such opportunities when they come along. Is it too ludicrous to suggest that if we must spend time in prayer to equip ourselves spiritually, time in study to equip ourselves intellectually, that we also need to take time for making money to equip ourselves financially to do God's work? I think not, although the idea may take some getting used to by both clergy and parishioners alike.

If making money could be seen as a divine calling, the church could be delivered from fainthearted leadership and the believers better equipped for the work of ministry. But before we can even think of making money as part of Christian spirituality, it is important that we examine wealth itself from a biblical perspective and absolutely crucial that we understand it grace-fully. We must develop a healthy attitude toward it, or we can never become responsible caretakers of what God entrusts to us. From the one to whom much is given, much will be expected. Yet before the "much" can be shared graciously, the "much" has to be seen as a blessing.

So what is the gospel with regard to money? What is the good news concerning wealth? Unfortunately, the church has more often than not been embarrassed by the question and changed the subject by mumbling something about laying up treasures in heaven where moth and rust cannot corrupt nor thieves break in and steal. The implication is that there is something sinful about earthly treasures. The gospel has been interpreted as having to do with souls, salvation, and sanctuary with God in a life hereafter. The church has, in fact, spiritualized our faith. The emphasis has shifted from the kingdom of God to the kingdom of heaven; from Jesus as the Son of man to Jesus as the Son of God. The focus has changed from social justice to personal sins, and concern for this world to attention on the next.

Dietrich Bonhoeffer, noting this tendency, warned Christians not to pass too quickly through the Old Testament on their way to the New. The New Testament needs to be understood in the light of the Old. Indeed, unless we take note of Old Testament earthiness as we pass through its landscape, we shall not recognize the new creation when it breaks upon us in the New.

A case in point: Jesus' words, "Blessed are the peacemakers, for they shall be called the children of God" (Matt. 5:9). When most believers hear those words, they immediately think of a person who reconciles differences; a peacemaker: one who builds bridges across disagreements. And when we think of God's peace, if we think of it at all, we assume that it refers primarily to peace of mind. God's peacemakers are people who possess a beauty of spirit and exhibit remarkable calmness in crisis situations. Such beautiful people are called "sons and daughters of the Most High" because they transform conflict into calm.

But this is probably not what Jesus had in mind at all, and Bonhoeffer's warning might have slowed us down long enough to note the Hebrew tradition out of which Jesus came and spoke. The Hebrew word for "peace," is "shalom." In the Old Testament, shalom was used as a greeting and a farewell, but it had far more significance than a simple "Hello" or "Good-bye." Shalom was a divine blessing. To bless someone with shalom was, in fact, to ask the Holy One to grant that person everything needed to experience the goodness of life in all of its fullness. For example, shalom could refer to a person's health: "May

14

you be blessed with good health and your days be long upon the earth. Shalom!" It could refer to a person's prosperity: "May your flocks multiply and be so numerous that your wealth will be great and you will have more than enough to pass on to your children. Shalom!" It could mean security: "May your borders be secure and your relatives so numerous that in your old age you can be assured of loving care for as long as you live. Shalom!"

Of course, "shalom" could also mean peace of mind. But Old Testament Hebrews recognized that peace of mind, in no small measure, came from having access to the good things of life. Material possessions were regarded as the blessings of God's providence. God's creative intention was for people to enjoy the fruits of the earth and rejoice in their abundance and goodness. This understanding was conveyed in the single word of divine blessing, "Shalom!"

All of us, I imagine, have experienced shalom. Yesterday I was working on our family's finances. When I finished writing the checks to pay all the bills and told my wife what she had left with which to buy groceries for the month, a great cloud descended over her face and threatened to engulf the entire McClelland household. If not weeping, there was at least much gnashing of teeth. Life seemed bleak and the future looked grim at best. If that brings a smile to your face, it is a knowing smile. You have been there. But it was no laughing matter yesterday. Then my daughter brought in the mail and among the envelopes was an insurance check reimbursing us for some dental work that had been done, and about which I had forgotten. That money meant financial solvency for us and reinforcements for our beleaguered checkbook! My wife had more to live on, and that fact alone, produced a decided change in her outlook on life. The clouds lifted, the sun appeared, and the basic benevolence of the universe was seen. That was an experience of shalom. It was the sense of well-being that came, knowing we could make it. Nothing spiritual about it. It was mediated through cold hard cash: dollars and cents.

There have been times when my wife and I barely had a dime between us. There have been other times when we had money in the bank. We can live, as could the apostle Paul, in either state. But I can say quite honestly we like having money more than we enjoy being without it. I dare to believe such a response is not a perversion of faith but an affirmation of the Old Testament recognition that material well-being is a blessing, not a curse.

Returning from a funeral some time ago, I was thinking about the tragic nature of the death, fully impressed with the frailty of life, and aware of my own finitude. The sense of life's shortness and uncertainty left me in a pensive, if not depressed mood. I was grateful for the noise of traffic and the pulse of flashing neon signs that made me aware I was in the mainstream of life again. That, too, is the experience of shalom!

A painting or a piece of sculpture to which my psyche responds can engender a sense of well-being and wholeness in me. It conveys shalom because it makes me feel good to look at it or hold it in my hands. Spirit speaks to spirit. Similarly, when the sound of great music plucks the strings of my soul and I am once again awakened in the depths of my being to the mystery and miracle of life, I am invigorated. Shalom!

The relaxing contentment of a back rub, the blissful satisfaction after making great love, the enjoyment of a gourmet dinner; all of these are manifestations of shalom. There is truth in the cartoon that portrays a little girl sitting on a mountain of candy saying, "Chocolate is my life!" It may not be traditional theology or even good dental hygiene, but it touches a responsive cord in the heart of every true chocaholic, and is probably why gifts of candy and flowers are given on special occasions. They add zest to life. They convey shalom.

I enjoy investing in the stock market because, for me, it has been a form of recreation, like playing Monopoly for real. As a parish minister, there have been times when I felt like Charles Atlas carrying the weight of the world on my shoulders with the wolves nipping at my heels. Investing provided a very relaxing diversion for me. Some nights when I had trouble going to sleep because of a worry or problem I had taken to bed with me, my wife would whisper, "Think about your stocks." In no time, I would be fast asleep. That is shalom. And I want to add that when the stock market is up, I am a better person because I feel better about myself. I am a better minister, writer, father, and lover. I feel more hopeful, joyous, and alive—that is shalom also.

Now the problem is, although all of us know something of shalom, we are afraid to trust our experience. We have allowed an external authority to label it for us as "sinful." It is almost with a sense of confession and some embarrassment that I tell you I feel better about life and myself when the stock market is up. I feel guilty about such an admission and worry that you will think I am less of a "Christian" because of it; that I should put my trust in the Lord.

These feelings of guilt are generally felt by Christians who are trying to take the high road to spiritual maturity, but they are particularly acute among the church's clergy. As a professional group, we are frequently reluctant to negotiate salary increases or admit to our congregations the desire for financial security. We think it unbecoming to a person of faith. We are victims of the myth that ministers are spiritual leaders who ought not worry about such things. Sometimes we "bad mouth" money. There is the subtle envy for a colleague who, though no more deserving, commands a better salary than we. We may say disparagingly, "Oh, so-and-so is in it for the money," as if doing the work of a minister for nothing made it worth more in the eyes of God, as if voluntary service was somehow more ennobling. We tend to compare ourselves favorably to, or make judgmental comments about, a colleague who, if he or she only worked harder, would have more to show for it in terms of a larger church membership if not a bigger salary. And at the other end of the spectrum, we take a certain perverse pride in being workaholics ourselves, thereby earning our worth and convincing ourselves and others that we are deserving of admiration if not monetary remuneration.

The advice sometimes given by church leaders to its loyal sons and daughters who are slugging it out in the front-line trenches does not do much to alleviate our anxiety about money. For example, the board of pensions of one of the mainline denominations recommended for reading by all of its ministers a book on finances that warned,

> As a minister, your lay constituency will look askance if you show too much interest in the stock market. There will be talk about your readership of a financial publication and it is never wise to study the stock listings in the newspaper in public. Such small matters do often affect a minister's influence on the community and sometimes his salary."[1]

The attitude that this advice embodies is all too typical of the church's views on wealth and its accumulation.

My guilt as a clergy person in sharing with you the sense of well-being that adequate wealth gives me is typical of the attitude all believers have when it comes to a discussion of personal salaries and family income—at least in public. These are private matters and no one else's business. Such attitudes are both unfortunate and inappropriate, given the Old Testament's perspective on wealth. But it typifies the hang-ups believers frequently have about money. It is tragic but true: Our faith has made us suspicious of worldly possessions as if they were sinful rather than equipping us to enjoy them as blessings from God. We have interpreted Christian living more often as self-denial and the suffering servant than as the enjoyment of life.

There is good reason why our faith has made us feel guilty about wealth. The history of Christian theology has been stained with an antimaterialistic bias. During the very earliest days of the church, believers moved out from the hub of Jewish culture, along the spokes provided by the trade routes of commerce, into the Greco-Roman Empire. There they encountered the dualistic world view of Greek thought. When life is looked at through a pair of these spectacles, anything of a material-historical nature is seen as inferior when compared to the nonphysical realm of mind and spirit. The former is subject to decay and corruption, while the latter is immune to such blights. This dualistic split between mind and matter, spirit and substance, provided the church with the intellectual framework for interpreting the gospel to the world. Since, in the scheme of things, God and the devil are opposing forces, we can see how God, quite naturally, came to be associated with the realm of mind and spirit. This world of substance, on the other hand, was destined to be seen as the arena of sin and Satan. The enjoyment of material things could only stand in the way of the believer's spiritual development. God was understood as a spiritual reality "without body, parts, or passions," as the early creeds put it. And if you, yourself, wanted to become godly, you set the alarm early so you could leave your sleep on a straw mat and get started on your prayers. Certainly, you canceled your subscription to the *Wall Street Journal*. In other words, the religious ideal became monasticism, in which taking vows of poverty and chastity were the surest ways of getting this world off your back.

Because of this antimaterial bias, the church, understandably, interpreted such stories as Jesus' dealing with the rich young man (Matt. 19:16–22) as a summons to sell worldly possessions and a call to humble poverty—an interpretation that misses Jesus' humor and the point of the story. The punch line has nothing to do with eternal life nor the command of Jesus to "Go, sell!" Rather, it is focused in the invitation "Come, follow!"

The young man in Matthew's story had asked what the requirements were for eternal life. It was a bad question because it assumed that salvation was something he could earn like a trophy to be added to his collection of other admirable accomplishments. As his response to Jesus indicates, he believed salvation could be found by perfectly fulfilling the obligations of God's law. But Jesus answered his bad question with an obviously absurd answer, an answer designed to show the ambitious young man the impossibility of ever being saved, given his assumptions about life. Jesus said in effect, "If you want to be perfect, keep all the commandments."

We must remember that Jesus had just redefined all the commandments in such a way that it is obvious no one can keep them (Matt. 5:21–30). To commit adultery, according to Jesus, is not simply going to bed with someone else's spouse, but even thinking about it. Similarly, to kill is not the act of murder itself, but merely being angry with the other person. Nevertheless, the confident youth claimed he had kept all the commandments. He thought he was well on his way to perfection and smugly awaited Jesus' commendation.

Instead, Jesus, with a twinkle in his eye, decided to teach him a lesson. "If you really want to be perfect, that is, if you really are serious about going this route and earning a heavenly reward, try this com-

18

mandment on for size: Go and sell all that you have and come follow me." Given his mind set, the fellow took Jesus seriously, and as Matthew describes the scene, "When the young man heard this he went away sorrowful; for he had great possessions." We all fall short at some point and that is what Jesus wanted him—and us—to understand. Trying to earn divine grace is an exercise in frustration and futility, and it is totally unnecessary. Grace is freely given. The story, therefore, has nothing to do with the evils of wealth, much less the advantages of poverty.

Jesus, of course, did speak of the special problems wealthy people have with the kingdom of God. It is harder for them to get in than for a camel to pass through a needle's eye (Matt. 19:24). Possessions can possess us, so we must take his warning seriously. But Jesus himself had an eye for the finer things. When the invited guests to the wedding in Cana ran out of liquid refreshments, he provided the finest champagne so the celebration could continue in style (cf. John 2:1–10). Obviously Jesus enjoyed going first class and wanted everyone else to enjoy the best as well.

On another occasion a woman came up to Jesus and opened a jar of very expensive lotion with which to anoint him. One of the excited disciples declared in righteous indignation, "Stop her! It's an extravagant waste. Sell the ointment and give the money to the poor" (cf. Matt. 26:6–12). A noble idea and, had we been there, one with which most of us would have concurred. "Amen," we would have said. Not for benevolent reasons born of concern for the poor but because we have a conditioned knee-jerk response to religious ostentatiousness. But it did not seem to bother Jesus. "No," he said, "leave her alone. She is doing a beautiful thing. The poor you will always have with you."

The church has never known quite what to do with his response because it runs counter to traditional expectations and offends our dualistic understanding of spirituality. It is ironic that this puritanical strain of faith stems from religious ancestors who affirmed, in the Westminster Catechism, that the chief purpose of human existence is to glorify and enjoy God forever. Yet we have been infected with this antimaterialistic bias that focuses attention on the glories of the life to come rather than the preciousness of the one at hand. As a result, we skip lightly over the very biblical assertion that the things of this world are good because God created them that way. They are, after all, to be understood as gifts of God's grace. When Christian spirituality is not rooted in the Old Testament, it tends to produce deformed, spiritualized fruit.

This unfortunate spiritual schizophrenia is summarized by a bumper sticker I recently saw, "Jesus saves, but Moses invests." Christian concern is limited to the salvation enterprise and has become a spiritual matter having to do with heaven. This world is left to the devil, or some form of social gospel, but in any case, it is assumed to be well on its way to atomic or environmental ruin if not going to hell in a handbasket. This early disparagement of having and holding wealth, much less enjoying it, is echoed in the contemporary concern for our economic relations with Third World nations. It has become fashionable in some circles of Christian thought to blame the United States for most of the economic ills of the world, especially those of the developing countries. The effect is to heap more guilt upon ourselves for being Christians living in the wealthiest nation on earth.

Of course, there is a good bit of evidence to substantiate the case against us. The United States *does* fund military dictatorships that deny human rights and engage in torture and repression in order to support American investments abroad. All too often we discover the CIA has been involved in clandestine operations ranging from training mercenaries to organizing coups. American business interests certainly have been guilty of payoffs to corrupt government officials and collaboration with dictatorial regimes in South Africa, Brazil, and Korea. All is done with a fair amount of hypocrisy, misinformation, and propaganda; and all is done with a view to bottom line profits that can be reported at the annual shareholders' meeting.

But it is too simplistic to label the United States as the villain who stands in the way of a utopian destiny for these nations, as if they were solely the victims of American colonialism. If American influence were removed from the scene entirely, the brass ring would still not be within the grasp of the vast majority of the world's population. This country has no corner on greed. Many developing countries are ruled by wealthy elitist governments that remain unconcerned about the suffering masses in their lands. Repression, intimidation, and violence have become institutionalized and sanctioned by vested interests in both church and state. The nation's wealth is held by a very few who own a large percentage of the best land and produce export crops to earn foreign exchange. They continue to live in luxury while the majority of their country's citizens face grinding poverty and starvation. Marcos of the Philippines, Samosa of Nicaragua, and Noriega of Panama come to mind as only the most recently exposed and blatant examples. Nevertheless, when we characterize Uncle Sam as the "bad guy" and point the finger of blame at this country, the net effect of this oversimplification is to heap guilt upon ourselves as American Christians and make us feel personally responsible for the plight of our economically oppressed brothers and sisters.

Ironically, the interest of many mainline churches in Third World liberation theology often seems to be rooted in, and fed by this sense of guilt. Grounded in the biblical concept of divine justice, which portrays

God as the champion of the oppressed, Latin American Christians have recovered for all believers the worldly dimension of spirituality. Yahweh opposes the greed of the pharaoh who would keep economic and political freedom out of the reach of God's people. God advocates their cause before the power mongers of the world and leads them in revolution against the state. Those who would oppose the people's deliverance from economic and political bondage are crushed, as God bulldozes a pathway to freedom for them through the wilderness.

While it is certainly important to hear the concerns of these economically deprived and politically oppressed members of the human household, the sense of guilt regarding worldly possessions that their cry engenders immobilizes us for any immediately effective personal response to their plight. This theological viewpoint implies, if not states, that the Christian ethical imperative demands we divest ourselves of what we have. "Go, Sell!" It assumes that our wealth is sinful. Our power and possessions are curses that not only dehumanize the disadvantaged people of the world but will destroy our souls and lead us into perdition. Oddly enough, both liberal social action theology and fundamentalist theology seem to be in agreement on this point.

The difficulty with such an assessment is twofold. First, it is hard to peddle in Peoria. The rich young man in Matthew's story was not buying and neither are most of us. Selling all that we have is not a spirituality that many Christians will be moved to adopt. Not because of hardened recalcitrance, but because our experience with shalom does not convince us that it is more godly to be poor than wealthy. Our experience does not convince us that we are better off sick than healthy or happier insecure than when we are secure. As a result, the theology of guilt with its imperative to give everything away is simply not convincing.

Second, a spirituality that opts for a more simple lifestyle based on poverty does not really get at the problem. Giving all our wealth away may be a heroic gesture, but it ignores both the problem of poverty and the possibilities of possessions. Changing our lifestyle and eating fewer bananas just because they are tainted by the greed of United Brands may salve our consciences, but it does nothing to solve the problem. It only aggravates the situation. Andrew Greeley, novelist, priest, and sociologist argues that even if "our guilt finally becomes too much to bear, and we decide to reform . . . [informing the peasants in] the fruit orchards of Central America that we can dispense with bananas in our diet . . . their joy will hardly be noticed as massive unemployment and depression sweep those countries."[2]

As American Christians, therefore, we seem to find ourselves with no good alternatives. We find ourselves in the unenviable dilemma of being "damned if we do and damned if we don't." Because of our exposure to Third World thinking, we come out on the short end of the stick. The accusation is clear enough: We are the enemies of God! We have no future in God's plan. We are the ones to be crushed as the oppressed are freed. God has abandoned our cause and stands four-square against us. The Advocate of the oppressed champions those who are the victims of our structured, institutionalized violence. The hope of the world rests with the preference of the Holy One for the underdog. We have been cast off by God.

That there is an economic imbalance is clear. What is not as clear is what to do about it. The problem with liberation theology is that there is no room in it for us as affluent Western Christians. The net effect is that we are left with massive feelings of sinfulness and despair, but it offers us no usable spirituality. We must either wait for the revolution to come, or confess our guilt and do penance by selling all we have and distributing it among the poor.

While such a theology is no doubt a necessary and healthy development in the reflection of Third World Christians on their situation, giving them, as it does, a usable future and a sense of identity, it offers little or nothing to us as First World Christians. Our response as Western Christians to the plight of our oppressed brothers and sisters must be something more creative than to roll over and die or to take vows of poverty. Instead, we must develop a theology of wealth—a shalom theology—one that sees possessions as blessings showered upon the earth and, as a result, to be shared by all people.

Before we change our lifestyle, therefore, and condemn our possessions as things of the devil, we need to reclaim our experience of shalom, accepting the joy and peace such possessions can, and do in fact, bring us. We need to trust our experience and hold our wealth in open hands as a gift of God's grace. Life's good things are to be enjoyed because they are good. Quoting Bonhoeffer again, "It is only when one loves life and the earth so much that without them everything would be gone, that one can believe in the resurrection and a new world."[3] And with all of its bumps and warts, that goes for the fruits of American free enterprise as well.

At the first assembly of the World Council of Churches held in 1948, delegates from Europe and North American were preparing a document condemning one of those fruits—technology—for its debilitating effect on human life. They were stopped by a comment from Bishop Rajah Manikam of India. "Before you condemn technology," he pleaded, "will you, please, let us have it in India for fifty years."

Viewing our situation from a shalom perspective invites us as Western Christians, to look at our wealth, our technological capabilities, and our influence as God-given means for enhancing human life. These things can, and do, provide us with a sense of well-being, which we have come to call a "good life." They can bring peace of mind, provide a measure of security, enhance happiness, and contribute to human well-being and health. Of course there are inherent temptations and dangers in having and holding wealth, but rather than seeing our resources as a curse, a shalom theology moves us beyond our incapacitating sense of guilt and calls us to see them as blessings of divine providence that convey to us, and to others, the goodness and wholeness of life. The spirituality that a shalom understanding of wealth engenders is a radical sense of stewardship, a responsibility for sharing these gifts with others precisely because we see wealth as a possibility rather than a liability.

In our world, money has power—power to do good, power to educate dulled minds, power to fill empty stomachs, power to shelter the homeless, power to heal broken bodies, power to bring justice to the disenfranchised, power to share the light of the gospel with those who dwell in places of deep darkness. In a monetary economy, dollars make sense as a vehicle for the grace-full distribution of shalom to all the earth's inhabitants. When Jesus says, "Blessed are the peacemakers," we need to understand what he meant. He was not praising those who settle quarrels. His use of the word "peace" was drawn from the religious culture of the Old Testament. "Blessed are the shalom makers." He was not talking about calming people's nerves nor reconciling differences between them. Those may be very worthy ends but they are not what Jesus had in mind. As a good Jew, he was talking about shalom and calling his hearers to be shalom makers.

His invitation has our address on it. Because of our location in time and space it has, for us as Christians living in the United States, a particularly relevant ring. It comes with a promise. Shalom makers are the ones who will be called sons and daughters of God because, like God, they are the ones who shower the earth with shalom. Our location in history carries with it an invitation to be one of those created in the image of God who share the abundance of life's good things with the world; things labeled "good" by no less than their Creator.

Chapter Two

Sharing the Much

When we open the Bible, we discover a spirituality spread on its pages that has a great deal to say about wealth and the people who own it. Unfortunately, the antimaterialistic bias of the church has contaminated our reading of the text so that we have come to believe the word of God sees riches as a liability rather than a possibility. An example:

> The land of a rich man brought forth plentifully; and he thought to himself, "What shall I do, for I have nowhere to store my crops?" And he said, "I will do this: I will pull down my barns, and build larger ones; and there I will store all my grain and my goods. And I will say to my soul, Soul, you have ample goods laid up for many years; take your ease, eat, drink, and be merry." But God said to him, "Fool! This night your soul is required of you, and the things you have prepared, whose will they be?" So is he who lays up treasure for himself, and is not rich toward God. (Luke 12:16–21)

The usual interpretation of this story speaks of it as a teaching concerning the folly of a life devoted to the accumulation of material wealth. It is ridiculous to seek security through riches. The foolishness becomes obvious, so the interpretation goes, when that very night the man suddenly dies and must stand before God. Then he sees with tragic clarity the utter folly of it all. It was stupid, if not sinful, to amass riches. The reason drawn from Jesus' words for not accumulating material possessions is that we can become trapped in desires for them. We can be hooked on the comforts of a materialistic world. Better, therefore, to be spiritually rich and economically poor.

This interpretation suggests a fair amount of projection into the picture of our situation. Never mind that neither wealth nor materialism was a big problem for Jesus' listeners. Poverty was more the order of the day. A wealthy middle class is a relatively recent sociological development. The one person out of every 425 in this country who is a millionaire must be seen as a new kid on the block, certainly not present in Jesus' congregation. Nor has it been true, unfortunately, in any of the congregations I have been privileged to serve. Happily, for my ministerial colleagues in the state of Idaho, I understand the millionaire ratio there is one out of every four. In any case, the conventional wisdom on the text argues that rather than accumulate wealth and material possessions, we would be better advised to spend our time in spiritual pursuits, i.e., becoming rich toward God.

The trouble with this traditional interpretation of the text is that it, again, does not square with our experience. Many people enjoy working. True, our labors bear fruit and provide income. But some of us find great satisfaction and pleasure in the challenges and rewards of work. For us to deny our gifts and abilities would be to deny who we are: our identity, our very being. Some of us do not find working and, therefore, the accumulation of those things that come as a result of our endeavors, to be evil. Furthermore, as we have noted, those things do, in fact, bring shalom. Possessions do enhance our lives. Our experience leads us to conclude that money has the ability to bring blessings to ourselves and others; it has the power to do good.

Because our experience does not square with the traditional understanding of Jesus' parable, we fail to take the story seriously. We manage to feel guilty, of course, because most of us are affluent by this world's standards and assume the bony finger of accusation is pointed at us by Jesus. Yet we do not really believe that riches are evil or that the satisfaction we derive from our work is blasphemous. Consequently, when we give money to the church or charitable causes we do so dutifully, perhaps grudgingly, but out of a sense of obligation and guilt.

Church stewardship campaigns understand the dynamic of this motivation and frequently seek to tweak our consciences with pictures of people in dire straights—hungry or homeless—as if we were not already aware of their plight. The appeal is to our sympathy, a subtle form of guilt for being better off than those in need; but seldom is it a call to respond out of joy.

Our difficulty with the story, however, may not be an indication of stubborn sinfulness so much as it is an indication, born of our experience, that the conventional interpretation misses the point.

The most memorable line in the story is the oft-decried admonition to "Eat, drink, and be merry," for tomorrow you may die. The underlying assumption among believers is that there is something wrong—cynical, if not sinful—about eating, drinking, and being merry in the face of death's certainty.

Such a conclusion flies in the face of the religious tradition out of which Jesus came, however. His spirituality was one that emphasized celebration and feasting. Clearly Jesus enjoyed a good party. We have already noted, when attending the wedding reception at Cana, he saw to it that there was plenty of good wine for everyone—120 gallons by John's count! That must have been some party!

Later, he was carried away when feeding the multitudes by the sea and, after everyone had eaten their fill, there was enough food left over to fill twelve baskets with doggie bags.

Many of Jesus' parables about the kingdom of God draw on his own experience at dinner parties. And let it never be forgotten that his critics found sufficient justification in his lifestyle to accuse him of being "a glutton and a drunkard" (Luke 7:34). Jesus was clearly a person who enjoyed eating, drinking, and being merry.

The story, therefore, deserves another look.

On closer examination, we discover that Jesus did not condemn the man for eating, drinking, and being merry, nor even for being rich; instead the man was called foolish for building bigger barns. The entrepreneur was planning to store more of his wealth than he needed to eat, drink, and be merry. Look again at the words of the story. The man says, "What shall I do for I have nowhere to store my crops?" Not true! He has barns. His problem is that his harvest has been so great that his present storage facilities will not hold all the grain. So he decides, "I will tear down my barns and build larger ones, and there I will store all my grain. Then and only then will I have ample goods to eat, drink, and be merry." Again, not true! He already has ample goods. He does not have to live in the moment. He has barns for his future. They may not be as big as he would like, but he has plenty to eat, drink, and be merry. The man already has enough wealth to enjoy shalom. He has a sense of well-being and security because God has generously blessed his land with fruitfulness. Fortune has smiled on him, and he has been able to accumulate a sizable portion of this world's goods.

The point of the story is not that the man was wrong to amass some wealth but that he was intending to build bigger barns and store it where it would do no one any good. Its shalom capabilities would be lost. He was called "foolish" because he did not realize that his wealth had brought him shalom blessings and that it could do the same for others if only it were not locked up in those bigger barns. His sin was not that he had become wealthy, but that he wanted to hoard all his wealth. His sin was not that he ate, drank, and was merry, but that he was withholding the means for others to do the same. He had become a bottleneck in the flow of shalom blessings to others.

If, as I intend to suggest later, a monetary point in Jesus' parable of the talents (Matt. 25:14–30) is that we are to risk making money to the glory of God, then the point of this story is that we are to share the profits of that risk with others—to the glory of God. The story, so understood, is not a teaching condemning the foolishness of gathering wealth; rather it condemns the refusal to share the wealth we do not need. It warns about the shortsightedness of failing to be good custodians of the abundance God entrusts to us.

Now that is a story with some relevance for us as Western Christians and one we need to hear. You and I can eat only so much. Our closets can hold only so many clothes. We can live in only one place at a time. It is possible to draw the line at some point and say, "We have enough." Yet our society has moved beyond the production of basic human needs to become a "consumer society" whose vitality and growth is maintained by convincing us that we need everything: a second car, an electric toothbrush, a new boat, a vacation home, a closet full of new clothes every time fashions change. Government officials take great pride in pointing to an expanding economy, but it expands only by selling us goods and services we do not need. We are a nation of bigger barn builders.

We are citizens of the richest nation on the face of the earth; 6 percent of the world's population. Yet we consume 40 percent of its resources. And still we cherish the illusion we are a charitable nation, with a big heart, offering a helping hand to anyone needing a lift. The statistics, unfortunately, portray reality in a different light. Of all the Western countries, the United States ranks fifth from the bottom in percentage of gross national product shared with other nations. We rank behind Sweden, the Netherlands, Norway, Denmark, Australia, France, Belgium, Canada, New Zealand, the United Kingdom, Germany, and Japan.

Another fantasy we have about ourselves is the notion of our Christian generosity. A few years ago, one mainline denomination proudly reported it had given in excess of $2 million for the relief of world hunger. That figured out to be about 88¢ per member, not even enough to buy a Big Mac.

Now I use these statistics not to add to our sense of guilt which, as we noted earlier, is considerable, but to cause us to consider our situation. Individually, we are, by any world measure of wealth, affluent people. I may not have great wealth, but measured by this world's standards, I have much wealth and it brings me and my family shalom. It enables me to eat, drink, and be merry most of the time. I certainly feel more secure with it than without it. It brings a sense of well-being, more than if I were poverty-stricken. I do not mean to suggest that people on welfare cannot find happiness. It is just that I do not wish to trade the problems of wealth for those of poverty and I know of few who do. Nothing brings shalom like a roof over your head and three square meals a day.

Furthermore, I have not stolen my wealth. I have not raped the world for it nor do I need to feel guilty about having it. Yet collectively we seem to be a bottleneck in the flow of shalom to the rest of the world. Something is preventing everyone from enjoying the cornucopia of divine blessings. Jesus' parable, therefore, does have relevance.

As a believer, I am now faced with a crisis of faith. How am I to regard my wealth, and what am I to do with it? Sensitized to the plight of the world's oppressed peoples who are my brothers and sisters in Christ, and aware of the blatant institutional violence inflicted on them by my country's colonial interests in which I as an American citizen play a role, I must now make a choice. Either I can feel guilty about being wealthy and dispose of my goods as a danger to my spiritual health or I can regard my wealth as a blessing showered on me for no more reason than the rain that falls on the just and the unjust; yet nevertheless to be used in the service of the Holy One.

To state the choice this way is to suggest neither that faith in the providence of God is a guarantee of material prosperity nor that material possessions are a sign of divine favor, as if being poor was a sign of God's displeasure. The theology of "good guys win and bad guys lose" is a quid *pro quo* understanding of life repudiated by the Old Testament book of Job and the New Testament understanding of grace. Indeed it is just this understanding—or more properly—our inability to understand God's grace, that lies at the heart of life's mystery. Why are some blessed with health and happiness, not to mention wealth, and others are not? The question both puzzled and bothered the psalmists of old. It is still a contemporary quandary. Why are some born on this side of the tracks, or ocean, or border, and others are not? The very concept of grace makes us aware of the mystery of our good fortune, on the one hand, and our need for humility and gratitude for what has been given to us, on the other.

Yet, although questions arise regarding my wealth as a divine blessing, I am not delivered from the crisis of decision about its use. A worldly spirituality confronts me with a choice. If I regard my wealth as a mark of sinfulness about which I should feel guilty and for which I need to atone, then the ethical imperative is clear. Danger: Confess, and sell it! If I regard it as a gift of grace that brings shalom into my life, the imperative is equally compelling. Amazement: Give thanks, and share it! What we think about our wealth is the basis for our ethical response regarding it. A stewardship of guilt and obligation emerges from the former; a stewardship of gratitude and responsibility from the latter.

To see my possessions as blessings from God is to realize I have them on loan. I cannot possess or own them. A blessing is not something I earn, something for which I can take credit as if it was part of the cause-and-effect scheme of things. We have no ultimate claim on our blessings—otherwise they lose their grace-fullness. That I have them at all is a gift of grace that defies rational explanation. Why I, as opposed to someone else, should have been entrusted with them is a mystery. But that they have been entrusted to me is a fact I cannot escape. That they be put at God's disposal, therefore, is required. It is clear, I do not hold title to them. I hold them in trust. They have been lent to me, left in my care and keeping for a time.

John Claypool recalls a childhood story that illustrates this graceful understanding of possessions.

> When World War II started, my family did not have a washing machine. With gas rationing and the laundry several miles away, keeping our clothes clean became an immensely practical problem. One of my father's younger business associates was drafted and his wife prepared to go with him and we offered to let them store their furniture in our basement. Quite unexpectedly they suggested that we use their washing machine while they were gone. It would be better for it to be running, they said, than sitting and rusting. So that is what we did, and it helped us a great deal. Since I used to help with the washing across the years, I developed quite an affectionate relationship with that old green Bendix. But eventually the war ended and our friends returned and, in the meanwhile, I had forgotten how the machine had come to be in our basement in the first place. When they came and took it, I was terribly upset and I said so quite openly. But my mother being the wise woman she is sat down and put things in perspective for me. She said, "Wait a minute, son. You must remember that machine never belonged to us in the first place, that we ever got to use it at all was a gift so instead of being mad about it's being taken away, let's use this occasion to be grateful that we had it at all."[4]

Shalom theology understands wealth in this way. To say that God has left some possessions with us for a time is to say that God has put us in charge of them and their use. We do not own them, but we are responsible for them.

Though biblical, this is a radical concept of stewardship because it claims any hungry person has as much right to the bread in my freezer as I do. The shirt hanging unused in my closet belongs to anyone who needs it. The money that I plan to bank must be held in joint ownership with the poor. To say that my wealth is a blessing that brings shalom is to say in the strongest possible way: Everybody and anybody in need has as much claim to it as I do. I do wrong to everyone I could assist but fail to help.

Keeping that realization before us makes clear our role as custodians to whom much has been given and of whom much is required.

A shalom theology makes three affirmations about the much.

1. **The much is from God.** Wealth, as we have said, is a blessing from God and can bring shalom into our lives. It is not sinful.

2. **The much is sacramental.** Wealth as a blessing is to be seen as a sacramental sign of God's love and trustworthiness. Its significance lies in directing our attention beyond itself to the Giver who stands behind the gift.

I am always delighted whenever I run across a lucky penny. Maybe it is the little boy in me. Certainly it is not the amount of money. But whatever it is, when I find one it is, for me, an indication of the divine presence close by. God has passed this way. No matter where the path leads, I can trust God's guidance for my journey. It is as if the Holy One were hiding somewhere in the shadows, watching, enjoying my surprise.

Annie Dillard tells a childhood story of occasionally hiding a precious penny of her own for someone to find, just for the excitement of it.[5] She recounts how she would draw big arrows on the sidewalk leading to it and label them, "Money ahead," or "This way to a surprise." Then she would watch from her hiding place, waiting for somebody—regardless of merit—to find her free gift of grace. She observes that the world is fairly strewn with lucky pennies flung broadside by some generous hand in the universe.

What a grace-full way to regard pennies—and dollars! Lucky pennies are sacramental reminders of God's smiling presence. As sacramental signs, our dollars point not to themselves as something to be held tightly, but rather beyond themselves to the trustworthy God who has strewn them in our path and hides in the shadows enjoying the shalom they bring us. To confuse the sacramental sign with the thing signified is what the Bible means by idolatry. Hence, to clutch our dollars as if they were ends in themselves rather than seeing the hand that has cast them broadside in our pathway, is to become an idolater. Therein lies the danger of wealth about which the Bible is so concerned. But the danger does not diminish the sacramental function of wealth, which is to remind us of the One who hides along our pathway. When we understand money sacramentally, we can see we are directed by our very wealth to trust in the God who feeds the birds of the air and provides fantastic fashions for the flowers of the field. God's provide-ence is secure; currency is not. It can be devalued, lost, or stolen.

3. **The much is to be shared.** Wealth brings shalom into our lives and, consequently, is to be shared with others because it has the power to bring shalom into their lives as well. The right to private property is not an absolute. From a biblical perspective there is no such thing as private property because, as the psalmist says, "The earth is the LORD's

and the fulness thereof" (Psalm 24:1). The world's treasures, therefore, are God's and we are merely stewards of them for a time.

Property owners in the Old Testament did not have the right to harvest everything in their fields. They had to leave some for gleaning by the poor. But more significantly, when Israelite farmers purchased land, Levitic law held that they really bought only the use of the land for a period of time until the jubilee year required its return to the original landowner. The Old Testament ideal of a jubilee year was intended to provide an institutionalized way of assuring economic justice in society. It was poor people's right to receive back their inheritance at the time of jubilee. Returning the land was not a charitable courtesy that the landowners might extend if they pleased. It was a required understanding built into the ownership and, consequently, the stewardship of land.

Similarly, the biblical practice of tithing provided a structured way to remind the owner that all wealth belonged to God and offered the giver a systematic way of sharing its blessed benefits with others.

With the elements of a shalom theology before us, let us examine in more detail the structure of sharing.

Early Christians saw this sharing as part of their spirituality and a mission of the church. Ronald Sider describes how the early church structured itself to be a community of shalom makers.

> The earliest church did not exist on absolute economic equality nor did they (members) abolish private property. Peter reminded Ananias he had been under no obligation either to sell his property or to donate the proceeds to the church. Sharing was voluntary, not compulsory. But love for brothers and sisters was so overwhelming that many freely abandoned legitimate claims to private property. No one said that any one of the things which he possessed was his own—that does not mean that everyone donated everything . . .[6]

What it does mean is that the early community of shalom makers sought to limit the liability of wealth and practice total availability of possessions. They tried to enflesh the shalom understanding of wealth and its radical implications in their lifestyle. Their attempt is worth a second look because it makes a financial spirituality functional. It moves us in the direction of a structured stewardship that makes shalom a possibility for others.

So, let us return to the story of the prosperous farmer who had to make a decision about building bigger barns to hold his surplus harvest. Again, the central point is that the rich man had plenty of barns for holding his ample goods to eat, drink, and be merry. He did not need bigger barns to hold more goods. The story would have a different ending if the man had recognized this fact and shared his surplus with others. He might even have been spoken of by Jesus as "rich toward God." But as it stands, the story addresses us as affluent Western Christians.

Let us hype the point of it by supposing we are millionaires. Now that is a consummation devoutly to be wished! But probably not a present prospect. Nevertheless, it is a fantasy worth entertaining for a moment.

If you had a million dollars, what would you do with it? Specifically, how would you change the world? I find that an intriguing question. It is, in fact, the question of shalom stewardship because a million dollars is more money than most of us need to eat, drink, and be merry. That we are now able to live on our present incomes would seem to suggest we do not need much more. Some, perhaps, but for the most part we have enough. We are able to make do; able to eat, drink, and be merry. Everything between our present income and a million dollars is surplus wealth. Consequently, if our dream came true and we inherited a million dollars from a rich uncle, we would suddenly find ourselves standing in the shoes of the rich man about whom Jesus was speaking. We would have more than ample goods and, like him, would be faced with the question of what to do with them. What are we to do with our overabundance? Do we build bigger barns to store our wealth even though we do not need it? Or do we try to change the world a little because we believe in the power of wealth? Do we share the surplus with others—thereby, enabling them to eat, drink, and be merry—because we ourselves know firsthand something of the possibilities of wealth? Or do we put it in the bank?

What about a half a million dollars? Or even a quarter of a million? Would there be any surplus money after expenses for eating, drinking, and making merry?

Of course your present income may not be adequate for your present or anticipated financial needs. You may have children to put through college and graduate school. Or you may have aging parents to care for. But at some theoretical point on a monetary continuum it is possible to draw a line and say, "Enough! I can live with this amount and fulfill my responsibilities and financial obligations." Everything beyond that figure, whether it be a million dollars, a half million, a hundred thousand, or a mere fifty thou—whatever—everything beyond that point is surplus and can be given away without jeopardizing your own shalom.

The relevant points for us to glean from Luke's story, therefore, seem to be at least the following:

1. Like the rich farmer, who had much, all that we have is to be received gratefully as a blessing from God.

2. Nevertheless, there is some level of wealth that is ample for us to eat, drink, and be merry, just as there was for him.

32

3. Unlike the rich man, however, we understand ourselves as stewards entrusted with our wealth for a time. We are not merely to store it away but to put it to good use as the Spirit of God indicates. We are to share our surplus with others in direct proportion to the abundance of our blessing.

A worldly spirituality invites us boldly to examine our financial resources and declare at what level we have enough. We do not have to squirrel more and more of our wealth away in bigger and better barns or savings accounts. There is some level at which each of us can say after cold sober reflection, "I have ample goods. Thank you, God!" Beyond that level Jesus invites us to consider sharing everything else with others.

The spiritual discipline of radical stewardship cannot be taken lightly. If we believe that our goods do, indeed, bring us shalom, then

INCOME	(✔)	TITHE %	TITHE GIVING	GOD'S MONEY
$20,000				
21,000				
22,000				
23,000				
24,000				
25,000				
26,000				
27,000				
28,000				
29,000				
30,000				
31,000				
32,000				
33,000				
34,000				
35,000				
36,000		10%	$3,600	$1,800
37,000		15%	150	75
38,000		20%	200	100
39,000		25%	250	125
40,000		30%	300	150
41,000			$4,500	$2,250
42,000				
43,000				
44,000				
45,000				

we must recognize that they can also do the same for others. For that reason we are called upon—as good caretakers to whom much has been given and of whom much will be expected—to share the much with others. The alternative is to view all that we have as a curse, endangering our souls and, therefore, to be abhorred and rejected completely.

The value of shalom stewardship is that it can offer a structured means by which we state what is for us enough wealth to eat, drink, and be merry, and a systematic way for sharing the surplus with others through a graduated tithe.

Let us suppose, for example, that a single person could live comfortably, if not luxuriously, on $20,000 a year. And let us suppose further that each additional person in the family requires an additional $4,000 to make ends meet. Using these hypothetical figures, a couple might find $24,000 ample for their needs while a family with three children would require $36,000 as their level of "enough-ness." The following table provides a systematic way for such a family to figure a graduated level of giving on a salary of $40,000.

Now, try your hand at filling in the table by using your figures.

1. Locate with a check (✔) the basic level of income that fills your family's needs. Let me suggest that you begin thinking in terms of $20,000 for a single person plus $4,000 for each additional person in the family. Obviously, this figure may be higher or lower than your particular requirements.

2. Tithe this checked (✔) figure at 10 percent as a reminder that all your financial blessings come from God and are only entrusted to you as a steward for a limited amount of time.

3. Tithe each additional $1,000 of income above the basic level at an increasing rate of 5 percent per $1,000. In the example offered, the basic level of need for a family of five is $36,000 ($20,000 plus $4,000 x 4). The tithe on this amount is 10 percent or $3,600. If, however, this family's income is $40,000, then each $1,000 above the $36,000 is tithed at an increasing rate of 15 percent, 20 percent, 25 percent, etc. The total shalom giving for this family would be $4,500.

4. Pledge half of this amount ($2,250) to a church where it will be assigned to its shalom use by church officials. But consider designating the other half as "God's money." Once God's money has been set aside, it remains only for the Spirit to indicate how it is to be given joyously and recklessly away to others. You are its sole custodian and, therefore, enjoy the adventure of working more intimately with God in its use than is possible through institutional giving. The enjoyment comes back into giving because the money has already been set aside. You have the makings of your own private foundation. It is money looking for God's assignment and you are privileged to see both the need and the results firsthand.

34

Chapter Three

Decisions about Dollars

Our reaction to the exercise in shalom stewardship called for in the last chapter may be revealing. Any uneasiness about letting go of our wealth puts us in the sandals of the rich seeker spoken of in chapter one. We can clearly see in the story told by Matthew that in the critical assessment of Jesus the rich young man lacked only one thing. He was obedient in every other regard, but he could not respond to the invitation to "Come, follow" because he was owned by his possessions. When the word of the Lord came to him, he was closed to it and "went away sorrowful" rather than plentiful, because his possessions meant more to him than discipleship.

The poignant retreat of the rich man in the face of Jesus' invitation to "Come, follow" poses a disturbing question for many of us. Can affluent Christians hear the word of God? Can a church that is secure financially, or strong statistically, offer anybody a word of salvation?

The great danger inherent in riches, about which Jesus warned, is that it tends to make us arrogant possessors of wealth and insensitive to human need. For example, our nation's economic and legal system is stacked in favor of those who have wealth. If you have cash or a secure job, you can get a good credit rating. Having a good credit rating gives you access to the goods and services of this world. Unfortunately, if you do not have cash or a secure job, you cannot obtain a good credit rating and, therefore, have no claim on the goods and services that others do. In our society, human need is not the central concern of economic justice as it is in the Bible. A person's access to economic opportunity and legal justice is all too frequently based upon net worth, not intrinsic human dignity.

Wealth has a tendency to make us Americans arrogant. That arrogance is justified by what we have come to call "the Protestant work ethic." Its logic is simple: Since work produces, it is good. And since God likes good people, God rewards those who work. Unfortunately, the same logic works in reverse: because unemployment does not produce, it is bad. And since God does not like bad people, God punishes those who do not work. The end result is self-righteous arrogance. Wealth is evidence of God's benevolent approval, and poverty is proof of God's righteous indignation. In the age of industrial revolution, when economic laws were assumed to be as real and certain as the law of gravity, it became an article of faith in the creed of American free enterprise. Bright, ambitious people deserved to be well fed and dressed, while others, who might be classified as "dull" or "lazy," deserved nothing but the crumbs from the blessed table of the prosperous or their discarded clothing offered in charitable rummage sales.

Given our predilection to read the economic tea leaves as signs of God's pleasure or wrath, we are genuinely surprised and truly affronted when accosted by the biblical assumption that riches can be a real stumbling block to those entering the kingdom of God.

Wealth has the capability to convey shalom, but it also has a nasty way of creating its own needs. The more of it we have, the more we want. We never seem to have enough. As a result, gaining wealth tends to become an all-consuming concern. Often we become victims of our desire to get ahead and never take the time to live, enjoying family, friends, or health. The miracle of a sunset eludes us because at the moment we must get some reports out before going home. The softness of a child's touch is missed because we are out hustling to stay ahead of the competition. The wisdom in a chance comment of a friend is lost because, given the task at hand, it is "irrelevant."

Even more serious is the subtle temptation lurking in the shadow of the well-to-do, to put our trust in the power of money. We credit wealth, rather than God, with the ability to bless us. Not only are we not amazed by divine grace, we feel no need of it. Money and power become the objects of our faith. We trust their ability to fulfill our heart's desires and solve all our problems. God gets a polite tip of the hat on Sunday and at supermarket openings.

As we have seen, divesting ourselves of all wealth is not the spiritual remedy prescribed by scripture. Tithing is.

In the Old Testament, the discipline of tithing was a required understanding that accompanied the holding and, consequently, the stewardship of wealth. It was not intended as a means of raising money, later to be replaced in the Christian church by the Christmas bazaar or Friday night Bingo. Its purpose was to remind the holder of wealth that when we are not possessed by our possessions we are more open to God. The spiritual rationale for fasting and the observance of Lent by giving up something served the same purpose.

This does not mean that selling what we have and giving it to the poor makes us more acceptable to the Holy One. It is not the financial status of our wallet that makes us more or less noteworthy in God's eyes. It is the divine image inscribed within our humanity—rich and poor alike—that God recognizes and loves. Giving away all that we have and heading for the desert, therefore, does not go down in God's book as a meritorious act. Jesus' command to the rich young seeker to sell everything was a specific and personal prescription for him. However, the general malady that both infected him and endangers us, is one of hearing. Those who are tied to their possessions are deaf to the word of God.

In story after story the Bible affirms that those who carried the divine promise were landless people with no place to lay their heads. The Old Testament story of Abraham and Sarah affirms that the bearers of Israel's covenant promise were wandering, landless nomads living in tents. The call to freedom was not heard by the pharaoh who, with all of his ambitious economic plans, lived in established security and suffered, the record contends, from arteriosclerosis of the heart. It was Moses who heard God's call, but not in the courts of the pharaoh's prosperity. It came to him as a fugitive hiding in the desert. The disciples of Jesus were all men who turned their backs on the professional demands of work along with the possibility for advancement and its accompanying status and salary. They were willing to leave behind all such matters but there was nothing wrong with their hearing. They all heard the call of God.

Some might call their behavior a lack of ambition. Some might even say they were irresponsible. The Bible does not argue. It simply says, "Of such is the kingdom of God." In story after story, it seems to assume that if we are attached to our possessions, or committed to the path by which they are obtained, it is almost impossible for us to hear the word of the Lord. It is easier for a camel to go through the eye of a needle than for a rich person to enter the kingdom of God.

It is not that the Bible exhibits an inherent and malicious bias against wealth as such. Rather, it makes an observation about life. Those who are well off do not have to come to grips with life and, therefore, do not have to come to grips with God. It is no coincidence that the great artists of history have tended to be people who were hurt, either physically or psychologically. In some way, they have been torn open and, in the ripping process, have been forced to engage in that dialogue with life that produces great art. It is through such painful dialogue that great theology is also produced. That magnificent Old Testament book of Job was not written by the landed, wealthy Edomite sheik of the first chapter, but the broken, bloody pulp of a man sitting, bankrupt, on his dung heap. He had been caught by the whirlwind and, because of the encounter, left for us a written legacy of eloquent grace.

Out of this dialogue with life, which cannot be evaded, earnest prayer is forged. This is why it is so difficult for wealthy people to pray; they are too secure. To be secure is not having to deal intimately with life, and therefore, not having to contend with God. When we are comfortable and safe, when we are well off, well fed, and content, we do not have to come to grips with the absurdity of life and the mystery of it all. I know of few who have begun, and sustained, a serious prayer life apart from trouble of some kind.

Looking again into the mirror of scripture, we see the Hebrews leaving behind their wilderness wandering where it had taken forty years to shape them into a people of the promise, crossing the border that made them one of the landed peoples of the Mediterranean basin. It was then that the nation, feeling sure of herself like a maiden rejoicing in her virginity, planted crops in the familiar sod and dwelt in homes with secure foundations. It was then that the prophets rose up like thunderheads above the plain crying, "You shall be exiled, Judah. You shall become a landless people and your sons and daughters raised as strangers in a foreign land." God's verdict fell with the pulverizing force of a sledgehammer. "You must be powerless because you are my people."

And when the dust of those apocalyptic battles had settled, there stood the prophets amidst those who had escaped the holocaust and the exile, those who could once again sleep securely in their own beds. There stood the prophets declaring that the future of God did not rest with the secure survivors, but with those poor devils disappearing over the horizon into exile. The divine promise would be fulfilled in those who had no home or hope. God's future lay with those who had been torn loose from all the secure anchors and set adrift in the flow of history where, once again, they could be shaped by the living Word.

Tithing, like the message of those prophets, reminds us that those who are not tied to their possessions are more open to God's word, more pliable than those who are encrusted by their security.

What happens to us when we become secure in the land? What happens to those of us who own our homes, have money in the bank, are secure in our jobs, know where our next meal is coming from, and are sure of ourselves? Are we not the ones for whom God becomes an option to be worshiped (if religion is your thing) or ignored (if it is not)? Charity toward the poor is seen in the same way. You can take it or leave it, depending on how you are feeling about it at the time.

The legacy of the Reagan years has legitimized selfishness. "Why do I owe my neighbor anything?" has become a respectable question. If you get your jollies out of taking baskets of goodies to the poor, well and good. If not, you are under no obligation to do so. Whether you give cheerfully or grudgingly is irrelevant. The poor can be overlooked because, after all, they will always be with you, and in any case, they have no inherent right to the "good life," which others can claim by virtue of their wealth.

The "God is dead" theology of the sixties was an inevitable consequence of an affluent culture. The suburban church frequently took on the characteristics of a religious country club. And it is interesting to note that in this country, so influenced by the "Protestant work ethic," that Protestants make so little of Lent, fasting, or tithing.

The German sociologist, Max Weber, noted that Calvinism— because of its belief in human sinfulness, i.e., selfishness, coupled with its call to frugality—fostered and nurtured a capitalistic economic system. Roman Catholic philosopher and theologian, Michael Novack, believes that capitalism works better than any other economic system because we are sinners. "I believe in sin," he said. "Socialism is a system built on belief in human goodness; so it never works. Capitalism is a system built on belief in human selfishness; given checks and balances, it is nearly always a smashing, scandalous success."[7] The two systems of thought have grown up together so well, in fact, that capitalism has become a quasi-religion in our society. No one dares criticize it for fear of being called un-American. Politics and religion merge in the creedal statements, "I own what I have." "I earned it." "It is mine to do with as I please."

Novack may be right. Capitalism may work because of human sinfulness, but never let us forget that human sinfulness and greed are under the judgment of God. American business exists purely and simply to make more profit this year than last. I know of no company that takes pride in submitting an annual report to its shareholders revealing mere business as usual. Each year it strives to show an increase in sales and profits. Businesses are self-serving. Despite the claim of a fast-food restaurant chain that it does it all for us, the fact is that if doing it for us did not prove profitable, it would change its motto and policy. Regardless of what advertising agencies and Chambers of Commerce would have us believe, greed is not the consummation of the kingdom for which Jesus and his followers prayed.

The Christian's scriptural source of wisdom, without hesitation or apology, asserts a nation that fuels its economy on greed—that is, at the expense of others' basic needs—is not only a nation under God, but also a nation under God's judgment. Amidst all the sloganeering and flag waving, it must seriously be questioned whether such a nation is genuinely concerned about meeting the needs of the economically oppressed.

It is with such a "Protestant" understanding of wealth that the biblical message collides. It says to people who are financially secure and know where their next meal is coming from along with the dessert, "The trick to living, my friends, is to travel light and to live on your land as if you had no land, to own your possessions without being owned by them."

The invitation to discipleship was turned down by the rich man for whom life had been good, and our literary imagination fills in the commentary on the gospel story. "Jesus invited you to come follow him, but you are not open to it. Your possessions have made you deaf to his call and hardened your heart to the tug of the Spirit. You have fallen in love with your wealth. You cannot give it up, and worse, you think it belongs to you instead of to God."

The story line in Jesus' parable of the talents (Matt. 25:14–30) calls for the money given the stewards to be risked precisely because it is God's money. The stewards hold it only in trust and will be held accountable for its use. Jesus' point keeps rolling off our Teflon consciences like water off a duck's back. People with possessions do not want to be reminded that those possessions are to be held in trust and continually laid before the throne of grace, available to do God's good pleasure. So, rather than live with that burr under our saddle we, like the rich would-be disciple, choose to turn away. We go on our way—and usually not, as he did, sorrowfully. We go on our way rejoicing; rejoicing in our good fortune; grateful to General Motors but not to God Almighty.

But the Bible stands there as stubborn as a rock, and every time we open it to read, we stub our toe on its assumption that all the resources of our lives come from God: the strength of our hands, the cleverness of our minds, the health we enjoy, and the possessions with which we have been blessed. God has loaned them to us in trust. We are stewards of these gifts of grace, and we are to use them whenever and however the Spirit indicates.

Stewardship is not an option for us. It is not something we can take or leave alone. We, as landed people, need to be intentional about our stewardship of wealth if, by the biblical understanding of life, we are to remain human. Developing a worldly spirituality is crucial for us if we are to remain open to God's word in any sense. Cultivating an attitude of stewardship, therefore, is not an option for us, it is a necessity.

Those of us who have trouble giving 5 percent of our gross income to the church, much less a tithe or 10 percent, are in real trouble. God's word, the Bible, holds up a tithe for our consideration as if to say, "It isn't just a matter of 5 percent or 10 percent, or even 15 percent. God wants it all!" If we have trouble letting go of 5 percent or 10 percent, to that degree we are possessed by our possessions. To that degree we are shut off from the word of hope and light that brings life and humanity. God does not care any more about my family than a family in India. No more about a college education for your children than the children of migrant farm workers. Tithing reminds us that we are called to be stewards and not possessors.

Tithing is a useful discipline for believers living in this most affluent nation; believers who are learning to be disciples. Though we may own everything, we are to live as though we possess nothing. Worldly spirituality calls us to be radical in our ownership. It calls us to live as stewards of our possessions rather than as owners. Owners develop hardness of heart. Owners develop closed-mindedness when it comes to the things of the Spirit. Owners can no longer hear, nor respond, to the word of God. And churches of owners can no longer offer a word of hope to the world.

Bonhoeffer points us in the right direction with his observation that the only real ethical question is how shall the next generation live? We are not just here to live and enjoy life. That is a good beginning, but if left at that, it becomes self-centered. We are also here to enable others to live and enjoy life. Because we know how pleasant a home with a freezer full of food is, the responsibility for sharing our blessings rests upon our shoulders. At times the burden seems heavy. We squirm because the crisis of choice is upon us.

The New Testament carries a story that, instinctively, we do not like. We sense its threat. It is the story of Ananias and his wife, Sapphira (Acts 4:32—5:11). They are the ones, you may recall, who sold their property, intending to give the proceeds to the church, but then tried to cheat God by withholding some of the profit. The decision had dire consequences because, when their "creative accounting" was uncovered, they both dropped dead on the spot.

Our revulsion concerning the story arises from two problems that we have with it. First, we sometimes hear the story as espousing communism—believers holding everything in common—and, since we have a knee-jerk reaction to communism, we dislike this story. Indeed, with a touch of misplaced genius, some interpreters have used the account to prove that communism does not work.

Luke, the author of the story, was not advocating any economic theory, much less offering a diatribe against owning private property. Luke's story, and his reason for telling it, has to do with decisions about dollars. Ananias and Sapphira did not have to sell their land. That was their choice and they had made it freely. Furthermore, after they had sold their property, no one told them they had to give the proceeds to the church for distribution to the needy. That, too, was their choice. The point of the story is that, having made those choices, they then lied to God about how much the land was worth and withheld some of the money. And that decision, the story insists, had dire consequences.

The other problem we have with the story is that we are repulsed by the idea of a God who would zap someone dead. Luke, of course, does not make that claim. It comes from a careless reading of the text. The story simply claims that they dropped dead when they were confronted with their fraud. If we were to understand the story psychoanalytically, we might say Ananias and Sapphira died of guilt feelings induced by the discovery that they had not played fair with God. But whatever the psychological autopsy might reveal, the fact remains: Decisions about our dollars have consequences.

We see Matthew making the same point in his story of the rich seeker who came to Jesus but who could not surrender his possessions in order to seize the opportunity of becoming a disciple. But unlike him, we are not being asked to sell all we have in order to follow the Master. Nevertheless, we are required to make some decisions about our dollars in the historical context in which we have been placed by accident of birth. Every day we make scores of choices about buying, consuming, and sharing. Every time the offering plate comes our way in a worship service we are again reminded that decisions are called for about our dollars.

To become a disciple of Jesus we have to make a decision. There is nothing automatic about becoming a Christian. We choose to become a follower of Jesus, and that decision inevitably involves our pocketbooks. Ananias and Sapphira made the decision to join the community of believers. Further, they decided to do something about their faith. Selling and sharing seemed like a good idea at the time. But then they had second thoughts and held back some of the proceeds. Their pocketbook had not been converted. And suddenly their story is Matthew's story, repeated—and our story, reflected.

So, tithing! The reason for it is not to raise money for worthy or benevolent causes, though, of course, it does do that. Rather it faces us with the crucial question that lies at the heart of Christian spirituality. "Who owns my life and my property?" The temptation is to bob and weave. "I can't afford to tithe. Not with inflation. Not with the house payments, kids going to college, the expenses of refinishing the basement. It's simply out of the question. I can't afford it."

I mean to suggest that the Bible offers an understanding, but unyielding ear, to our cry. It insists we can ill afford not to tithe. The decision has to do with our identity as Christians.

Our society's obsession with industrial growth and corporate profits has revolutionized every aspect of life and seeks to shape our identity as a consumer animal. Look through any magazine and feel the energy of the image makers as they proclaim their gospels. As persons, we are unacceptable unless we buy Ban deodorant, while Scope mouthwash holds the promise of reconciliation. Unless we buy Scott's Turf Builder and have a greener weed-free lawn, we do not really love our neighbor or our neighborhood. Women are not really liberated unless they smoke Virginia Slims, and our peace of mind is dependent upon Fixodent that holds our plates firmly in place while we drink our Old Granddad, a sure sign that we are one of the beautiful people. And nothing more, nor better, can be conceived of in this life than owning a Cadillac.

You may not recognize this person as the image of God, but it might pass as a fair reflection of the person in the bathroom mirror. It is the new you, envisaged and molded by a consumer society. All the advertisements raise a moral issue. Ads do not simply tell us what is available to meet our needs. They are designed to create those needs and sell us goods and services that otherwise we could very well do without. Decisions about dollars is a moral issue because while we are busy buying things we do not need, people are starving to death.

The decision of Ananias and Sapphira was to hold back and to pretend they were still Christians. The rich young man, at least, had the good sense to go away sorrowful. He knew he could not have it both ways. "You cannot serve both God and mammon," said Jesus. "If you try to save it all—your life and your wealth—you will lose it." Ananias and Sapphira tried to do it—and proved the point. Their split decision killed them. It literally destroyed their identity as Christians and anything else.

A worldly spirituality does not demand that we sell all we have. It does call us to responsible stewardship. Our decision about sharing the much reveals the state of our spiritual health.

Chapter Four

Risk Stewardship

The traditional understanding of Christian stewardship runs something like this: A person pledges a dollar to the church and that dollar is budgeted for expenditure in local program or mission outreach. In chapter two, I suggested that half of the family's tithe be given to the local church. The radical nature of such a proposal will not be missed by churchgoers who feel generous when they throw a dollar bill in the offering plate on Sunday morning as if they were tipping God for services rendered. The irony has been caught in the doggerel:

> I bought a pack of cigarettes,
> I paid two bits for gum,
> I threw a buck into the plate
> And prayed thy kingdom come.

Most churches would be delighted to have a membership giving at the rate of 5 percent of annual income. The trouble is, even at 5 percent, a dollar pledged, received, and spent by local church authorities is not much power. What is needed is a money multiplier, in which the dollar set aside for God's use is multiplied so that instead of having just the one dollar for sharing shalom, five or ten dollars can be employed.

With a grace-full attitude about money and a responsible sense of stewardship for sharing it, we are now ready to talk about multiplying money. In this chapter I mean to propose a "Risk Stewardship Fund" as an adventurous part of a financial spirituality. The purpose of the Fund is to generate a surplus of what we have referred to as "God's money," the half of one's tithe not given to the church but rather given away recklessly as the Spirit indicates.

Interestingly, there is a way of generating money that enjoys a biblical precedent. It is through the practice of investing. Not saving money—investing it. The biblical reference, of course, is the parable of the talents (Matt. 25:14–30). In this story, Jesus is talking about a stewardship of multiplication. Not a safe conservative stewardship such as most churches advocate—one dollar given, one dollar spent—but a stewardship of risk—one dollar invested and multiplied, so that five or ten can be spent.

The point of the parable seems to be that the art of living requires a willingness to risk. The stewards who risked investing the landlord's money were commended for their efforts, even though they might have lost it all and been left empty-handed. With full knowledge that they were risking the owner's wealth, they sought to multiply it for his benefit and use, and were rewarded with praise and the promise of greater responsibility. Unlike the security-seeking dullard who merely buried his money in the ground for safekeeping and was soundly denounced for his trouble, the others were held up by Jesus as examples to emulate. While the landlord assumed all the financial risks, the risk of the stewards was that of not being faithful to their trust, a faithfulness, it must be noted, defined by risk.

As managers of a Risk Stewardship Fund, we are not interested in saving God's money by burying it in the ground or locking it away in a bank. The intent of saving money is the conservation of capital, but the purpose of a Risk Stewardship Fund is to increase capital. Naturally, multiplying capital always involves the risk of losing it. But as the parable makes clear, it is the Landlord's money we are risking; not our own. A Risk Stewardship Fund uses God's money. If the Landlord wants it invested, we can take the risk with divine permission given in advance. Neither the gain nor the loss is ours for which to take credit or blame. Our responsibility is to be faithful servants who follow orders by investing the Landlord's money. Our privilege is to be faithful stewards of the Fund. Our compensation is to be entrusted with the delightful decision about how to give the proceeds away.

There are no guarantees in life, and certainly none in making money, so we cannot be foolish investors. It behooves us, as stewards of God's money, to be as wise as serpents and as generous as doves—to misquote the Master (Matt. 10:16). The degree of risk will vary according to the personality of the steward who practices investing, but investing is always a tension between two factors: safety and the potential for gain. The art of investing is to find the degree of tension with which you, as a steward, can comfortably live.

What are the investment possibilities? First, let us eliminate some. Passbook savings accounts, certificates of deposit, and money funds are not really investments. They may be useful vehicles for carrying your family finances, children's college funds, and the like, but not God's money. They are designed to help a person save money and secure capital but not to multiply it. Their function is to store money while the savings and loan institution or bank uses it to make a profit for its shareholders. You are, in fact, loaning them your money so they can invest it. They, of course, pay you a conservative rate of interest for the privilege of doing so, but putting the Landlord's money in one of these is like burying it in the ground, and that, said Jesus, is a "No, no!"

Real estate has often been suggested as a profitable investment. In the seventies it was. The housing market enjoyed a boom time, but in the eighties it has lagged behind other investments as a money maker. Some real estate experts believe those boom times in the housing market are gone for the foreseeable future because they were fueled by double digit inflation. Now that inflation seems to be under control, they argue, housing prices, and therefore profits, are less explosive. But even if the boom time of the seventies were to ignite real estate profits again, rental housing would still be a particularly inappropriate investment for clergy people. Owning rental property requires either a resident landlord or one who lives close enough by so that the property can be checked occasionally. If one is a minister, being tied to the land is inadvisable because it clearly could color considerations about moving on when the calling to do so comes.

Clergy people aside, unless the owner of rental property is a do-it-yourself fixer, maintenance can be a headache and its cost is likely to eat heavily into investment property profits. The only reason for buying and owning a house is if you want to live in it and call it "home." Psychological and aesthetic factors that go under the heading, "enjoyment of home ownership," are perfectly good reasons for anyone to buy a home, but they are reasons other than multiplying capital and consequently ought not be confused with investing.

Some people think of gold, silver, and diamonds as investments. We could add such things as art, antiques, stamps, and coins to the list. All of these may increase handsomely in value, but none of these are truly investments. Precious metals and gems are hedges against inflation or troubled times. Their purpose is to provide an internationally recognized medium of exchange independent of government supported currency. In times of world unrest and uncertainty they have a kind of doomsday value, but as a means of investing, they are not suitable because their value is determined by world events. Their increase in value tends to be tied to times of crisis.

Collectibles such as paintings, rare stamps, and valuable coins are not good investments either. Gathering them is a hobby, something that a person should enjoy doing for its own sake. But as investments they may not be easily turned into cash. They require a buyer. Tastes in art are hard to predict. The value of antiques varies. Finding someone who wants your set of coins or stamps may take time because advertising in the trade journals is cumbersome, and a dealer will only offer wholesale value.

That leaves the stock market. Actually a walk down Wall Street still provides a convenient way for the average person, and especially clergy persons, to make money. There are three reasons why this is so.

1. The mobility of most people makes the owning of stocks very attractive. Unlike real estate, a stock certificate can move with you, which means you are not tied to any geographical location. One-fifth of the population moves every year, but clergy people usually speak of their moves in terms of "God's calling." Consequently, when the call comes to move on in God's service, it can be evaluated on its own merits without having to give consideration to staying close to one's investment property.

2. Stocks are easy to buy, sell, and supervise. You need not visit them. For that matter, you need not even visit a stockbroker who does the buying and selling for you. Stocks can be bought and sold and information gathered about them as easily as picking up a telephone, dialing a toll-free number, and talking directly to a broker. And this can be done from anywhere in the continental United States, which means that your investment money is liquid. You can get it quickly should the need arise by converting your investments into cash. Unlike real estate and collectibles, there is no time lag between the decision to sell and the ability to do so. There are always buyers for the stocks you have decided to sell if they are listed on the major exchanges: the New York Stock Exchange, the American Stock Exchange, or the Over-the-Counter market.

3. There is plenty of good advice available, and since some of us have never taken a course in business or economics—and none of us are, nor do we desire to be, financial wizards or stock experts—it is very reassuring to have such advice so close at hand.

The best source of advice is a good stockbroker. A broker's experience can guide you in both the selection of specific stocks and the timing of their purchase and sale. Picking a broker is something like choosing a doctor, a lawyer, or a car mechanic, and probably ought to be done in exactly the same way, that is, by asking friends who are satisfied with the service they have received. The broker should be a person with whom you feel comfortable in working; not pressured, intimidated, or hurried into a decision—someone who makes you feel that you and your account are valued. Certainly you will want to avoid a broker who "churns and earns." When the primary interest is in trading your account, buying and selling like a gunslinger shooting from the hip, the only person likely to make money is the broker who is charging you commissions.

A good broker, on the other hand, is worth his or her weight in gold despite the claims of discount brokerage houses. Good brokers earn every penny of their commissions because they have access to information that is otherwise hard to come by. They can sense the market's mood. They are familiar with a stock's personality. Many times a broker has suggested waiting to buy or sell a stock because the price was moving in the right direction and waiting even a few minutes might be advantageous. When this happens, the commission is earned several times over. A good broker is like a dance partner. With the right one, the two of you can make beautiful music together.

Other sources of good advice are the free market letters that nearly all brokerage houses offer. By asking to be put on their mailing list, you can avail yourself of these market letters, which come once or twice a month and give a good overview of the way financial analysts view the market. In addition, they always include a list of specific stock recommendations that the letter suggests will accomplish certain specified goals. You can also subscribe to independent market letters that range anywhere between one hundred and five hundred dollars a year. But any good public library will carry them and you can avail yourself of their wisdom at no charge.

For these reasons owning stocks provides the most convenient way to multiply God's money in a Risk Stewardship Fund. In addition to being convenient, however, stocks have proved over the years to be better investments than risk-free government treasury bills or the gamble of gold. Over the last 118 years, the total investment return from common stocks, including both price changes and dividends—and fully adjusted for inflation—has far exceeded the real return on risk-free U.S. treasury bills and has dwarfed the real return of gold-bullion investments. This is the conclusion of a study of these three investment instruments since the year 1871 through mid-1988.[8] Despite the stock market crashes of 1929 and 1987, money put into stocks would have provided a staggering 7,548-fold total return after deducting losses of purchasing power due to inflation. One dollar invested in a broadly diversified portfolio of stocks in 1871 would have grown in real value to $7,548. By contrast, a dollar invested in treasury bills for the same period would be worth only $8.00 in purchasing power today. Perhaps most surprising of all, an initial one-dollar investment in gold would only have grown to $1.55, adjusted for inflation, over the 118-year period. The lesson for Christian investors is clear. Despite their volatility, only stocks provide genuinely meaningful returns over the long haul. Stocks, which have historically proved to be the best place for an investor's money, will continue to be so for the balance of this century and beyond.

Unfortunately for many believers, entering the stock market seems to be either an overwhelming task, or a way of making a killing on a friend's hot tip. It is neither. With the advice of a good broker and a clear plan in mind, investing in stocks can be quite simple and very different from going to Las Vegas in the hopes of making a fast buck. Investing is not gambling. Gambling is seeking money multiplication purely by chance. Investing is the increase of capital through intelligent speculation with known variables. Certainly the quest for maximum capital gains or even outright speculation is perfectly legitimate for investors. Aggressive investing can be fun, and those with a talent for it can reap large profits. But speculation relies on Lady Luck, who, as we all know, is notoriously fickle. For most Christians, and especially those who are developing a Risk Stewardship Fund of God's money, the primary reason for owning stocks is the development of financial gain over a long period of time, not by one or two throws of the dice. We are not talking about buying a lottery ticket in the hopes of making money. We are planning to make money through intelligent investing, and that, in turn, is based upon developing a reasoned plan with your broker and sticking to it.

Before buying a portfolio of stocks, the first and most important step is to decide what kinds of stocks are needed. What we buy depends upon having an investment plan with specific investment objectives. A plan gives us a structure on which to hang the advice of a broker, and investment objectives translate into the balance we should seek between risk and potential reward. As a generality, the potential for profit increases the more risk we accept. The willingness to take some risk is as essential to human growth and development as it is to making money, so a wide variety of considerations should figure in an investor's risk profile. Among them are age, current net worth, current income, prospects for future income, possible inheritance, and the financial demands likely to arise in the future based upon marital and family status. But the most important consideration should be our own temperament. No matter how rational it may seem on paper, you should never take more risk than you can comfortably live with.

Nonetheless, Christians, who tend to be conservative in financial matters, should consider that a refusal to take any risk at all can be just as damaging to one's long-term financial position as taking too much. Remember Jesus spoke in a disparaging way of the super safe steward's conservatism and his unwillingness to risk any of the owner's capital.

The fear of losing money has kept many a fainthearted steward from being faithful to the Owner's trust. It is one of the major reasons why Christians stay out of the market. But there are two kinds of fear—incapacitating fear that immobilizes us and keeps us from acting, and normal fear, fear of the unknown and untried. The stewards in Jesus' parable were frightened by the responsibility placed in their hands. After all, from those to whom much is given, much is expected. That kind of fear is normal and to be anticipated.

But one of the stewards was tyrannized by his fear and was consequently denounced. His fear became incapacitating. He abdicated his responsibility by burying his loan in the ground. The others—also frightened—refused to let fear reign as lord of their lives, and accepted the risks inherent in living as good stewards. They bore their fear and gradually it dissipated as the unknown and untried became familiar routine. They were lauded for their willingness to take reasonable risks in the face of fear and they were held up by Jesus as models.

Still we fear being a *poor* steward of God's bounty; we are afraid of losing God's money. What if we were to lose it—all of it?! It is the concern of all the stewards in Jesus' parable. What if our attempts to multiply God's money go down the tubes and our investments turn sour? What if we have another stock market crash similar to "black Friday" of 1929 or the "black Monday" of 1987?

Although only a few can remember the stock market crash of 1929, the massacre of 1987 lingers fresh in everyone's memory and continues to haunt even the bravest investor. Fortunes were lost in the panic selling. But panic is never a good reason to sell a stock. Few companies went bankrupt on that black Monday. American business was, fundamentally, in good shape. Their economic underpinnings remained sound. Clearly, most stocks were not overpriced, as the market rebound over the following months revealed. Stock prices plummeted because investors were dumping their stocks for whatever they could get for them, thinking, no doubt, that economic Armageddon had come. Panic, not economics ruled the day. As Franklin D. Roosevelt reminded us after the first economic collapse, what we have most to fear is fear itself. Had investors exercised a little patience and harbored even a little faith in the return of rationality to the market place, they would have weathered the storm. More important, had they been buying when everyone else was selling—as seasoned investors were doing—they would have been rewarded with handsome profits.

Patience usually pays off. Newcomers to the market often become discouraged if their investments do not immediately move upward and downright anxious if they decline. Like the length of women's skirts, stocks go up and they go down. They oscillate as they reach for higher or lower ground. Almost certainly they will go down in price after you buy them because you seldom can buy at the lowest or, for that matter, sell at the highest rate. Trying to time perfectly your purchase or sale is an exercise in frustration if not futility, and jumping in and out of the market, like a Nervous Ned, can lead to massacre due to the whipsaw action of stock prices.

Generally speaking, stocks, like fashions, go in and out of favor. They have a rhythm and cycle to them like so many other things in life. If you happen to buy out of rhythm, or at the wrong time in the cycle, patience is the only way to get your money back and turn a profit.

But even if a company is forced to file under chapter 11 of the bankruptcy law, it does not become worthless. Filing a chapter 11 does not mean the company is broke and will disappear from the face of the earth. Rather it means the company is seeking court protection from its creditors until it can get its financial act together. There are plenty of buyers for such stocks, investors who see them as interesting speculations. Texaco, the giant oil company, comes to mind in this regard. After filing under chapter 11, its stock actually increased in value. Even in bankruptcy there is plenty of time to get out of an investment without a total loss because of the speculators who will buy it, waiting to see what the last card will turn up. As long as there are buyers, the stock will be worth something, and you can get out with your shirt, if not your pride. Further, many companies that have filed under chapter 11 have come back leaner and meaner. In short, they have provided patient investors, who stood by them through the storm, with ample reward.

One of the concerns most frequently raised by Christians when selecting specific stocks to buy is the problem of conscience. "How can we avoid investing in questionable companies? For example, companies involved in armaments or in Third World nations where human rights are repressed?"

It is a legitimate concern but something of a red herring. Those of us who raise the question are, nevertheless, taxpayers, and our taxes go to support the military-industrial complex, not to mention a foreign policy that does, in fact, support governments in countries where human rights are repressed. The question, in other words, would be more forceful if we were consistent in our concern. When the question is raised by a tax resistor, then the answer is quite simple, "Don't! Since you are clearly opposed to any and all support of the military machine or the repression of human rights then, of course, you simply do not buy stocks in companies that are, for you, questionable." It is a matter of conscience and consistency.

But the question is also based on a misunderstanding. Let us suppose that Black Motor Company, in addition to the manufacture of automobiles, also produces tanks for the army. It is assumed that if you buy stock in the auto company, your money is going to support its military effort. In point of fact, the money you pay for the stock does not go into the company's coffers at all. It goes to the person selling you the stock. By buying the stock you are not supporting the defense industry or even Black Motor Company. Your dollars are merely being offered in exchange for a piece of paper that some unknown person is willing to sell you. The only time Black Motor Company gets any money from the sale of stock is when it issues new stock sold to the public for the first time. But even then the proceeds come from the underwriters of the stock issue rather than out of your pocket. Buying stock in Black Motor Company is similar to buying one of its used cars. The money exchanged does not go to the automobile company. It goes to the person selling the used car.

You could, of course, argue that by buying a new or used Black motor vehicle you are helping maintain the popularity of their cars and consequently supporting their value and price. In the same way, it could be said that by buying stock in Black Motor Company, you are contributing to its value by supporting the price of its stock. This price strength in turn would demonstrate the company's financial credibility to lending institutions should Black Motor Company ever want to float a loan to expand its manufacturing capabilities. But this argument introduces secondary factors whose numbers are legion. We could just as easily argue that by buying a new automobile from any automobile company we are contributing to the financial well-being of an industry from which Black Motor Company will reap benefits. By contributing to a healthy economic climate we are making it possible for Black Motor Company to flourish.

So, returning to the question of investing in questionable companies: Many denominational pension funds do not seem to be bothered by the question at all. This may be due to a lack of conscience on their part, but it may also be possible that they view ownership in such companies as a way of adding their voice to the decision- making process of the company and using it as a means of protesting company policies with a view to reshaping them. Several religious groups, both Protestant and Catholic, have filed shareholder resolutions at annual meetings and have gained the company's attention and public's interest through the news media, thereby focusing attention on a moral issue. Individual persons can do the same sort of thing by owning shares in these companies. By owning Black Motor Company stock, you are at least provided with a voice for your conscience to speak that you would not otherwise have. The question, therefore, may be answered by choosing how best to register your concern—to buy and vote or not to buy at all.

In a similar vein, some Christians have a concern about investing in, and thereby, supporting the whole capitalistic system of free enterprise. How moral is it to make a profit at someone else's expense? Aside from whether the question is well stated or not, the debate over the relative moral merits of one economic system compared to another is beyond the scope of this book. The spiritual reality is: We live in this system, and unless we are willing to leave it for another, or change it in identifiable ways, the matter seems to boil down to living in our society as best we can to the glory of God. Since we do have some measure of wealth, a down-to-earth spirituality behooves us to be as good stewards of it as possible.

Let us assume, then, that we have been good stewards and that our investments have yielded fivefold or tenfold just as they did in Jesus' parable. What then? What do we do with God's Money Fund?

Although Jesus obviously offered no specific advice on which stocks to buy for a Risk Stewardship Fund, he did give some guidance on what to do with the proceeds: buy memorabilia. One of his most quoted, and misunderstood, financial teachings reads,

"Do not lay up for yourselves treasures on earth, where moth and rust consume and where thieves break in and steal, but lay up for yourselves treasure in heaven, where neither moth nor rust consumes and where thieves do not break in and steal. For where your treasure is, there will your heart be also" (Matt. 6:19–21).

Whenever this text is cited, the focus usually falls on the word "treasures," and the point drawn is: Do not accumulate them. We have already been alerted to the church's dualistic bias that lies behind traditional interpretations of these texts and have opened up new possibilities for spirituality. We hope we can now read the text and see that it is not emphasizing the dangers of treasures, much less their accumulation. Rather, Jesus is concerned with the focus of our spending. The questions that it raises are: Where do we spend our money? Heaven or earth? And what is it we buy? Do we buy things of the earth, which thieves can break in and steal or moths and rust can consume, or do we buy heavenly things, which thieves cannot break in and steal or moths and rust cannot consume? Jesus' concern is not with having money or with making it. But what we spend it on is of vital spiritual significance. The problem with buying earthly treasures for ourselves is that they are vulnerable in a way that heavenly treasures are not, and, therefore, poor investments.

Jesus' advice directs us to the joy of spending money. But what, we ask, is a heavenly treasure and how do we acquire it?

Certainly he was not suggesting that we can take our wealth with us in a life after death as if we could pass it through customs at the pearly gates. But neither does the text give us any hint that Jesus was redefining wealth in any other terms than material. To say that he was talking about some kind of spiritual investment such as amassing virtues, is to drag into the reading that old bias that keeps haunting us. The text will not support it. Furthermore, grace is grace, and no amount of money or good works will earn divine favor or entry into heaven. Salvation is not for sale. We cannot buy it. Clearly, Jesus was not talking about life after death when he spoke of heavenly investments. But what, then, did he mean by "heavenly treasure?"

There is no need to make a difficult theological question of it. Instinctively we know the answer. We frequently speak of something very much in this world as being "heavenly." For example, "That meal was simply heavenly! It was out of this world. Absolutely divine!" A

Broadway show tune exclaims, "Heaven, I'm in heaven . . . when we're out together dancing cheek to cheek."

While we are eating or dancing or what have you, we are dimly aware that something very special is occurring, something even unique. But it is in the *remembering* of the occurrence that the definition of "heavenly" is given to it. The underlying meaning behind our use of the term "heaven" or "heavenly," is that when we remember the experience of eating, dancing, or what have you, we step into another reality. We are transported to another world, a world set apart and totally distinct from everything in this common and quite ordinary world.

Memories partake of heaven. Thieves cannot break in and steal them. Moth and rust cannot consume them. Jesus' investment advice is to buy *memories*. Money is for spending, not hoarding. And risk stewardship reminds us that God's money is for buying heavenly memories because they are the only investments absolutely secure enough to pay uninterrupted dividends for life. Heaven, at least in this text, is that collection or bank of memories from which we draw satisfaction, and which gives life its sense of purpose and fullness.

Memories give us an identity. Elderly people in the waning years of life need to reminisce. It is crucial for them to remember the stories that have shaped their lives and made them significant. Not to have a memory is to be lost in history condemned to wander through life without roots and little sense of continuity or purpose. Sam Keen tells a poignant story of such a person.

On a Saturday afternoon in early fall, I was domesticating, defining, and privatizing my private space, constructing a redwood fence around my back yard. A man in his early thirties passed while walking his dog, watched me for a time, and asked if he could help. He explained that he loved to work with wood and that he had little to occupy his time. I accepted his offer, but before I could tell him when I would be working next, he interrupted me. "There is something I must tell you now while I remember it. If I wait, it may be too late. I don't know." He went on to explain that several years before he had been injured in an accident in which a piece of metal had pierced the section of his brain that stores and controls memory. Immediately after the accident he had been rushed to the hospital with little chance of remaining alive, and less of retaining the ability to engage in rational thought. Somehow he survived and the long road of rehabilitation began. He had learned to talk again with scarcely any impediment, but he still had no control over his memory. At one time he could remember incidents from the ancient past, but could not remember what he had said five minutes before. At

54

other times he could remember the recent past, but not how he had been injured. Lacking a dependable memory, he could not hold a job nor plan for the future, in spite of his technical intelligence being largely unimpaired. I listened to his story with a growing sense of tragedy. We planned to meet on the following Monday and work on the fence together, but he never appeared. I imagine he found the slip of paper on which I had written my name and address, in his pocket, but could not recall how it got there. Nor did I seek him out at his home for fear of embarrassment of not being recognized. How could a friendship develop where there is neither memory nor promise?[9]

Jesus' investment advice seems to suggest it is equally tragic to spend money on things not immune from destruction. Clothes go out of style and end up in the rummage sale. A new car depreciates and needs repairs. Food is eaten. But a memory is forever.

The twelfth-century Persian poet, Sadi advised,

If of thy mortal goods thou art bereft
and of thy store two loaves are left,
Sell one and with the dole
buy hyacinths to feed thy soul.

All of us draw on that bank of special memories that feed the soul and make our lives significant. I remember the vacations that we spent together as a family. I suppose we really could not afford them on my father's salary, but looking back at them, I have to say they made a lovely bouquet of hyacinths. On special occasions we went to the ice cream shop on the west side of town to buy nickel ice cream cones. It was in the midst of the Great Depression, when one thought long and hard about spending a nickel and the joke was that the buffalo on it would limp from clutching it so tightly. We could not afford the occasional extravagance, but I am grateful that my parents bought those marvelous memories for me. Like spiritual food, they feed my soul.

Then there are the memories surrounding one of my students. Both of her parents were dead. She had made it through college and wanted to do graduate work in psychology. Unfortunately, she could not afford the tuition. My wife and I helped her through graduate school and, looking back on the expenditure, find it infinitely more lasting than the living room furniture we were planning to buy, but did not.

There is the middle-aged blind mother with a grown family that my wife tutored through high school and then supported through Southern Illinois University. That investment paid off in great memories for us as well as the woman. Through her determined efforts there came into being a sensitivity to handicapped students on that campus that affected not only the attitudes of faculty and administration, but the style of architecture and landscaping in a planned expansion of the campus. My, what a memory that is!

I suspect that when we stand before God and present the record of our days, the Holy One will not ask us if we have any sins to confess. The obvious answer to that question is, "Yes, of course!" and we all know it. Fortunately, both Jesus and God assume we are sinners. They know, even if we do not, that sin is as much a fact of human existence as the color of our eyes or the lines of our face. It is the risk we must take if we are to live at all. God's response, therefore, to our recital of sins is apt to be something like, "So what's new? Tell me something I don't know. . . . Like, tell me a story."

That will be the moment of truth. Then we will be forced to draw on our bank of memories. When God draws the bottom line across our lives, all we will have going for us are the memories that record the investment of our lives. Aware that our lives are "as a tale that is told," the psalmist urges us to live them wisely (cf. Psalm 90:9, KJV). Perhaps we will be able to tell a heavenly tale, a story which, at the very least, contains memories of interest to us. If we are bored with the tale of our lives, we can hardly expect anyone else to find it fascinating. Certainly not God.

God is a lover of good stories, and I should think for the divine Tale Teller to fall asleep while we remember and tell the story of our lives would be the ultimate judgment! Hell will not be a pit of eternal fire, but the terrible realization that God is bored. We have not only wasted our lives but God's time as well.

Heaven, on the other hand, will be seeing a smile on God's face and a twinkle in the divine eye, to know that the Holy One is delighted with our story. "Well told," God will say. "Well told, good and faithful steward."

Chapter Five

Creating in the Chaos

Up to this point our discussion of worldly spirituality has only been concerned with the individual person's stewardship of money as a means of sharing shalom. It has not dealt with corporate stewardship for shalom service, that is, the distribution of those tax dollars mentioned earlier. To do so is to be thrust into the political arena where we must face the lions; the questions about the meaning of rendering to Caesar the things that are Caesar's and to God the things that are God's. Faith calls us to do just that. We must face these questions as unflinchingly as did the early Christians, because in that arena decisions are made that facilitate or hinder God's creative initiative.

From the earliest days of the church, Christians have always expressed their belief in God as Creator, Maker of heaven and earth, indeed, a new heaven and a new earth. For fear of idolatry, Old Testament spirituality forbade the likening of the Creator to any earthly image. Nevertheless, the vision of God described in the Book of Ezekiel is a radical envisioning of the Holy One. The prophet shockingly focuses on God's sexuality and draws our attention to the divine loins! (Ezek. 1:27) Later we will consider the divine sexuality as it pertains to human sexuality, but for now let us explore its political ramifications. God's loins are aflame with generative power.

Creation is more than exploding stars, belching volcanos, and the evolution of species. Creating the heavens and the earth—and certainly, a new heaven and a new earth—has to do with the exercise of God's generative power. It is the exercise of imagination in visualizing possibilities and the expenditure of energy to realize them. Creation, in this sense, is a political act. Consequently, the believer's concern with politics is based on the biblical doctrine of creation.

Perhaps one of the reasons why traditional spirituality has had trouble mixing its politics and religion is its failure to emphasize God as Creator. Traditional spirituality has put the theological emphasis on God as Redeemer. Its concern is with sin and forgiveness, and preparing believers for immaculate life with a holy God. Indeed, it seems obsessed with personal sin and its eradication.

For the sake of the record, let us note there are other biblical models for understanding Jesus as Savior than the sacrificial lamb of God whose blood redeems our sinful nature.

For example, in the parable of the so-called prodigal son (Luke 15:11-24), Jesus tells of an adventurous lad who "comes to himself" in a far country and returns home without the benefit of a Savior. The young man, to be sure, has composed and rehearsed a confession of shortcomings and, in fact, tries to deliver his prepared statement to his father. But the father interrupts him. He has no interest in his son's confession. Sin is not the issue. Instead, the father wants to party with his son who was lost and is found, was dead and is now alive.

In this instance, the role the Savior plays is Story Teller, not Sacrificial Lamb. Jesus offers us a new story to believe about ourselves and God, a new story by which to live, one radically different from those told us by the authority figures of this world: parents, teachers, employers, clergy. Their stories speak of good and bad, success and failure, reward and punishment. Their stories are based on conditional love and acceptance. But the story told by the Savior is one that gives us permission to live our flawed lives as though they have been accepted by God. Accepted, that is! Not simply forgiven. With such an understanding of Jesus as our Savior, it is no longer necessary to think of God as Judge—albeit a merciful Judge—who must forgive our human shortcomings as if excusing our very existence were required.

Nevertheless, sin-forgiveness theology has become central in the life of the church and Christian spirituality. The focus of Western theology has been on God as Redeemer. God as Creator has been lost to view. Even when the creeds speak of the Creator, the tendency is to locate the divine activity in the past. "In the beginning God created the heavens and the earth. . . ." The telling of the story is reminiscent of a fairy tale's, "Once upon a time . . . ." "The beginning" is the time of primordial chaos, when there was nothing; and when God finished, there was everything. Whether the creative process took six days or six hundred billion years, the interest is scientific: How did the universe begin? How did we and the other animals and plants of creation evolve? Unfortunately, the end result pictures the Creator God as not only remote, but irrelevant, having the qualities of a fairy godmother who waves her magic wand, turning pumpkins into coaches, ant hills into mountains, and dust into ancestors.

A more appropriate understanding of the Creator is found in that simple, but exceedingly relevant, description offered by the ancient Hebrew writers: God stretching the canopy of the heavens over the earth—God holding back the primordial waters that threaten to inundate the world—God setting the boundaries for sea and dry land so that life can begin. In such a world view, there is a chaotic power with which God must contend. Through the exercise of creative imagination, the Holy One envisions something other than chaos. With sovereign sweat and muscular might, the Creator works to bring into being the imagined picture despite the opposing will and power of chaos.

One of Rodin's sculptures portrays this theological awareness. The magnificent piece in the Metropolitan Museum of Art is entitled *The Hand of God*. There is the hand, strong and sensitive, working with a lump of clay, fashioning a man and woman out of the inordinate, chaotic mass.

Interestingly, the Philadelphia Museum houses another of Rodin's works entitled *The Hand of the Devil*. The hands are essentially the same. Both are the strong, sensitive, long-fingered hands of an artist. But whereas the hand of God is fashioning form out of the lump of clay, the hand of the devil is idly working it, continually destroying any shape that appears. The clay continues to exist only as a meaningless lump. It remains a chaotic mass of nothing.

The biblical understanding of God's creative activity is to bring order—imaginative, beautiful order—out of chaos. To create is both to exercise imaginative vision and to use one's energy to shape a new reality. It means holding at bay the destructive power of chaos that resists the new ordering. Creation is a continuing activity. The Bible begins with God as Creator and ends with God's vision of a new heaven and a new earth. God's generative activity continues, therefore, in the present world.

This realization sets the ethical imperatives for believers. We are to behold the Holy One's imagination at work and share in God's creativity. Living in the new creation is a present responsibility for Christians. Upon every believer is laid the divine mandate: "Be creative, you who are endowed by your Maker with imagination! You who have been created in the image of an imaginative and creative God, come join the Holy One in landscaping a new garden."

All of us face the chaos of life and seek to bring order out of it in one way or another. Teachers organize their subject matter by designing some pattern of meaning and forming a course to present it. Parents work with their children to channel the instincts and energies of youth into a base on which to build adulthood. Scientists organize random bits of data into a hypotheses for testing. Architects bring order into empty space. We schedule our days in an attempt to bring order and efficiency into the myriad of claims made upon our time. And every person tries to interpret life in some meaningful way. Necessarily, we search for, and either find or create, some kind of purposeful interpretation of the raw data of our experience. It is essential to mental health.

Similarly, we see Jesus at work creatively ordering his life. But in him we see the divine intention that throbs through all his activities. When we look at Jesus, we see the creative Word become flesh. Note his healing ministry, for example. Jesus looked at a demon-possessed person and with the eyes of imagination saw that person as he or she could be. He saw possibilities despite the chaos of illness. Consequently, he designed a new reality. He cast out the demons and forbade them to reenter the person.

When we look at the crucifixion, we see Jesus locked in a life-and-death struggle with the forces that sought to destroy him and his mission. There we see, with terrifying clarity, the destructive power of chaos with which Jesus had to contend. There we begin to understand the agony and the ecstasy of creativity to which we are also called. It is a struggle, a power struggle, and requires the expenditure of energy to bring order out of chaos. Chaos resists ordering. It opposes imaginative shaping.

Creation, understood in this way, is inherently political because it involves the imaginative use of power.

In his *Moral Man and Immoral Society*, Reinhold Niebuhr points out that all people and all societies tend to be selfish and hypocritical. Imagine, for a moment, a volleyball game being played between two church teams. Let us suppose the teams are playing for the championship of the league and the score is tied. The ball lands close to the line. All the good Christians on one team swear the ball was out-of-bounds, and all the good Christians on the other team swear it was in-bounds. The difference in the call is born of subjective self-interest, which while sincere, alters perception of the situation. The game cannot continue without rules and objective referees to intervene and bring order out of the chaos.

Such parochial blindness is the chaotic power that surrounds us and with which godly creativity must contend in establishing the peaceable kingdom. Fair play is not built into the world. Nor is there anything automatic about justice. It is a creation of human imagination and effort. It comes as a result of contending with the chaotic forces of selfishness and hypocrisy that resist it. A just society can only be created by bringing order into the chaos of self-interest. Justice requires a balance of power so that those who have too much, have less, and those with too little are given more.

The problem is, as Niebuhr points out, that the chaotic forces of life want to maintain control. Suppose one of the volleyball teams was allowed to make all the close calls. Its decisions are binding. In the dispute cited earlier, how do you imagine it would respond to the protests of the other team?

People and institutions with power seek to maintain their privileged position by force, if not persuasion. They will always vigorously resist any attempt to change the present favorable imbalance of power. The hand of the devil is in their actions giving the appearance of working, but in fact, continually destroying any attempt to give shape to a new order of reality. The solution, Niebuhr contends, is that some kind of coercive power will be needed to create order and hold at bay the destructive forces of chaos.

When "law and order" is used in political rhetoric, it usually means protecting the property and prerogatives of the privileged. But the biblical meaning of "law and order" is to provide space for life to grow and develop. It is another way of saying that God creates by holding the chaotic waters of self-interest at bay so life can take place on the earth. Law is the order God would impose on the chaos of sin and selfishness lying just under the thin veneer of civilization.

Probably no words in American memory are more familiar or hallowed than these, taken from the Declaration of Independence:

> We hold these truths to be self-evident, that all men are created equal; that they are endowed by their Creator with certain unalienable rights; that among these are life, liberty and the pursuit of happiness.

It is interesting, however, that the words that immediately follow are not as familiar nor as hallowed. The next words in the document are "That to secure these rights, governments are instituted among men. . . ."

I take that to mean, the function of governments—the purpose of law and order—is to secure these rights for all people. Governments exist to ensure the right of all people to life, liberty, and the pursuit of happiness.

The enshrinement of the first set of words and the lack of familiarity with the second has led to the creedal belief in this country that all people are given an even start in life. Everyone has an equal chance at the pursuit of liberty and happiness. We all start from the gate with an equal shot at the roses. The ones who forge ahead show more initiative, drive, and determination. The ones with more get-up-and-go are the ones who naturally should stand in the winner's circle. Given such an understanding of the vision of our founding fathers, there is nothing more patriotic than the belief that smart, ambitious people should see the world as it is—overpopulated, polluted, headed for the worst depression of all time—and get to the well first, before it dries up.

Somewhere along the line we began to think of ourselves as a nation under God, which gave this belief sacred sanction and the status of an article of faith. It was enshrined by Benjamin Franklin in the immortal words of Poor Richard, "God helps those who help themselves."

Unfortunately, such an understanding takes no account of the factor of luck. Those who are lucky get to the well first. Those who are lucky know where the well is.

My eighteen-year-old son, home from college over Christmas

vacation, landed a job for the holidays. He made some money in the grand American tradition. But he was no more ambitious than anybody else. Just lucky. He had a friend who knew someone at the post office. His friend got him the job.

In St. Louis there is a world of difference between the education offered young people in the inner city and that provided in the suburbs. Teachers' salaries are different. The tax bases are different. The SAT scores are different. What looks like an even start is, it turns out, a long way from being equal because some are born on the right side of the tracks. Some have luck on their side. Others do not.

If we are to speak of a nation under God, we need to consult scripture rather than Poor Richard.

A particularly interesting story told of David in the Old Testament sheds light on our discussion (1 Sam. 30:18–25). David is a tribal chieftain or king, and one of his cities had been sacked by the Amalekites. Hostages had been taken, including the king's two wives. With blood in their eyes and vengeance in their hearts, David and six hundred of his men set out in pursuit of the Amalekites. But by the time they came to the brook Besor, two hundred of his soldiers were too exhausted to continue. It was decided they should stay behind with the baggage while David and the remaining four hundred warriors continued the rescue mission.

The Amalekites were overtaken and killed. We can skip over the details. David was able to recover all the stolen property and free the hostages, including his wives and those of the other men.

> David recovered all that the Amalekites had taken; and David rescued his two wives. Nothing was missing, whether small or great, sons or daughters, spoil or anything that had been taken; David brought back all.

It sounds like a happy ending. But, alas, there are those tuckered fellows back at the brook Besor. They wanted to get back their wives and property as much as the others. But by the time they reached the brook Besor, they simply were played out. They were too exhausted to cross it. They were as motivated as anybody else, but their genes were not strung together in the same way as some of their colleagues. They simply lacked the stamina to go another step further.

Now the plot thickens:

> David came to the two hundred men, who had been too exhausted to follow David, and who had been left at the brook Besor; and they went out to meet David and to meet the people who were with him; and when David drew near to the people he saluted

them. Then all the wicked and base fellows among the men who had gone with David said, "Because they did not go with us, we will not give them any of the spoil which we have recovered, except that each man may lead away his wife and children, and depart."

It should be easy for us to identify with the feelings of the triumphant warriors. As Americans, we are used to being victors, dictating the terms of settlement. "Those other guys didn't have what it takes; they ran out of gas. No guts, no glory, girls, or goodies!" We could have written the script. It is an instant replay of the old tape, "To the victor go the spoils." To the guys who knocked off early: nothing!

What makes this story so remarkable is the response of the king.

But David said, "You shall not do so, my brothers, with what the LORD has given us; he has preserved us and given into our hand the band that came against us. . . . For as his share is who goes down into the battle, so shall his share be who stays by the baggage; they shall share alike." And from that day forward he made it a statute and an ordinance for Israel to this day.

Clearly, David saw things differently. He saw that through a series of fortuitous events, God's providence had blessed them and, therefore, God should have the credit for the victory. Strictly speaking it was God's booty. None of them had a right to it. God was the Victor, and to the Holy One goes the spoils. Since none of them had a right to the spoils, David decreed that they would all share and share alike.

David saw that people are not born equal, and, as a result, do not have an equal shot at the pursuit of happiness. Some, for instance, can march in the desert heat for weeks while others can manage only a couple of days before they drop from exhaustion. The commander-in-chief saw that his rule must make a law that improved on the chance of creation; the lucky and unlucky accidents of birth. From his response we find a clue to his concept of government. Godly government must secure the right to life, liberty, and the pursuit of happiness for all people. Caesar, too, must render to God the things that are God's.

Unfortunately, neither morality nor righteousness can be legislated. The function of law is essentially negative. That is to say, law can only legislate against human selfishness, greed, and anger. Law cannot make me love my neighbor, much less my enemies. What it can do is keep me from expressing my hatred of my enemies and taking reprisals against them. It can prevent me from excluding my less lucky neighbor from the blessings of shalom. It can protect those guys at the brook Besor from my anger and selfishness.

The era of enlightenment in Western civilization, however, colored our concept of godly government. It brought with it an assumption that by the rational use of law, nations could erect single-handedly a veritable kingdom of God. The flow of history assured progress, moving, as it did, with the currents of human evolution. Optimism was rampant at the beginning of this, the "Christian century." Two world wars, a depression, and the threat of nuclear annihilation have tempered our enthusiasm. We have since come to realize that rationality can serve the powers of darkness as well as those of enlightenment.

This disillusionment about the inevitable possibilities of law and order should not have surprised Christians. The central symbol of our faith, after all, is the cross. It was the symbol of law and order and it was used to crucify the Son of God. The best, most civilized, most advanced and far-flung system of law that had ever been devised put Jesus to death. Romans put Jesus to death, carrying out the sentence of Roman courts in the due process of Roman law, in order to keep the *pax Romana*. The inescapable conclusion is that if the Son of God, in all his innocence, purity, and love of others was unjustly condemned and sentenced by law in the name of order, then law, whether civil or criminal, cannot bring in the kingdom of God.

One of the great champions of law and order was Adolf Hitler. In some of his early political speeches of the 1930s, he gained great support for his party by promising an end to street riots, foreign intervention, and economic decline—all through law enforcement. Nor can we forget that the "final solution" to the "Jewish problem" was carried out, quite legally, under German law.

The point to be gained is not that the law is evil or that politics is dirty and to be avoided by Christians. The problem is not with law, as such—although, clearly, there can be good and bad legislation. The problem rests with our expectations of its possibilities. Law is the lowest moral common denominator that the powerful will tolerate. Anatole France put it cynically, "The law in its majestic equality forbids the rich as well as the poor to sleep under bridges, to beg in the streets, and to steal bread."

Yet, while law may be the lowest common denominator of public morality, Christians, no less than others, believe in its necessity. Winston Churchill was correct in his observation that democracy is a terrible form of government, flawed as it is with massive inefficiencies. Still, it is the best that the human race has been able to devise thus far.

From the vantage point of the cross, we can see the disparity between the fantasy of expectations and the reality of results. For example, we believe that before the bar of justice all persons are treated equally. Fantasy! Reality is that blacks are routinely given higher bails, stiffer sentences, harsher prison treatment, and fewer paroles than members of other ethnic groups—all for the same offenses. Reality is that the poor suffer under the law while the wealthy remain relatively safe from detection of their participation in illegal activity or, if detected, can usually buy or pressure their way out of criminal prosecution.

Jesus was a victim of Roman law and order. He reminds us of its limitations and deficiencies and that our place as disciples is to stand beside him with all the other victims of law and order. Jesus spells the obligation out for us: "I was in prison and you came to me." And when did we see him in prison and come visit him? His reply: "As you did it to one of the least of these my brethen, you did it to me" (Matt. 25:36, 40) Jesus clearly identifies himself with the victims of injustice; and a worldly spirituality calls us not only to identify with them in personal, pastoral ways, but also to use the political means at our disposal to create in the land a law that raises the floor of morality for those who have been ignored or oppressed by it.

Unfortunately, people on whom Lady Luck has smiled tend to think the function of government is to protect their property and position. It is not that these folks are any more selfish than others, it is just that people who have been lucky tend to be out of touch with reality and to live in another world.

Before Ronald Reagan won his 1984 landslide presidential victory, he was questioned, during the campaign, about his net worth. It was rumored that, as an actor, he had accumulated a considerable sum. His wife, Nancy, stepped in somewhat defensively to answer the reporter's question: "Oh, we don't have all that much. Maybe two million. Others have much more." Obviously, she did not consider herself a "wealthy" person. "Wealthy" is a relative term and its meaning rests in the eyes of the beholder. Lucky people think differently than the majority of the world's population who are not so lucky.

It is precisely the cry of the unlucky ones, and especially those of the Third World, that calls into question the assumptions about wealth that we, as North Americans, hold sacred.

To be reminded of the relativity of such assumptions is risky business. After all, conservative politics and conservative religion sleep comfortably together. To challenge either is to be labeled a "Communist" on the one hand and a "heretic" on the other. As soon as someone starts talking about bringing our free enterprise system under the scrutiny of the international community, we feel a knee-jerk reaction that we call "patriotism," but which is nothing more than pure, unadulterated greed.

But a worldly spirituality must challenge the assumption that property is the sole possession of the person who owns it. The privilege of owning private property and passing wealth on to those whom we

65

designate through inheritance must continually be weighed on the scales of stewardship. Property rights are not articles of faith. A shalom understanding of God's good creation argues that essential resources belong to the entire community, whether local, national, or global. Those who control property and wealth, whether persons, corporations, or governments, are only stewards of God, holding it in trust as a gift of grace to be used for the shalom of the whole human race. In the final analysis, we are accountable not only to God but to the whole of humankind. It is the godly right of the community to assert its control of resources when they are being abused, squandered, or used to enrich a few. The right to the pursuit of happiness, not to mention the rights to life and liberty, move us away from the perpetuation of an economic caste system where wealth is passed on from generation to generation, from lucky ones to lucky ones. Christian stewardship, and, therefore, politics, may call for a return of private wealth and property to the community after the lifetimes of those whose luck enabled them to earn it in the first place. Millions of unlucky people, hungry and homeless, cry out for such an understanding of property and its inheritance.

Worldly spirituality must nurture a daring and imaginative social concern. It must call for nothing less than global consciousness. We cannot settle for an individualistic piety concerned only with souls and sanctification. Unfortunately, in the competitive climate of a free marketplace, it is assumed that each person and nation will—indeed, must—look out for itself and its own interests. The climate of rugged individualism carries over into the arena of religion.

Multitudes of our people look upon their spiritual journeys as a religious quest in search of personal fulfillment. The rise of the huge array of nondenominational parachurch organizations and Bible study movements that have captured the allegiance of millions, offers a personalized perspective of the gospel story that panders to this market. The emergence in the late 1960s of the charismatic renewal movement has further individualized the Christian faith. All these religious groups are aggressively seeking converts.

Even in mainline churches the emphasis today is on evangelism. But, unfortunately, evangelism's concern is with increasing church membership rather than confronting people with the claims of the gospel. The drive toward self-preservation is, in the end, stronger than the desire for social reform. Whether because of fear, tiredness, boredom, or change in the national temperament, the causes of the sixties have given way to different priorities. Virtually every public opinion poll comes up with essentially the same results: The concern for social justice and human rights is losing ground in the search for an individualized spirituality and numerical growth.

The story of Nicodemus comes forcefully to mind. Nicodemus was a middle-class, fairly well-to-do person of prestige and stature in the community. Yet with all of his comforts, he was vaguely uneasy about himself, sensing that something was lacking. He came to Jesus to talk religion; but certainly not politics!

Across our country an apparent spiritual revival is moving in the hearts of white middle-class Americans. A senior vice-president of New York Life Insurance Company, who found religion, summarized the feelings of many who have felt their hearts "strangely warmed." "Before, I wanted to be successful in the world; now I want to exalt the Lord. I want to stay a businessman, but I want people to know that God changes lives."

As middle-class Americans, we, like Nicodemus, feel a certain lostness and want a sense of certainty. And like Nicodemus, we hunger to know that God loves us, as we are, that God blesses us, as we are, and that God gives us permission to be as we are. "I want to stay a businessman, but I want people to know that God changes lives." Change lives, yes! But not society! Not New York Life Insurance Company. Not the system. Our brother wants to stay with the system. He wants to remain a vice-president in good standing with the company. Like Nicodemus, millions of us—comfortable, fairly well-to-do, enjoying some status in the community, well thought of by our peers— nonetheless come to Christ to talk about religion, hungry to know that God loves us as we are, blesses us as we are, and gives us permission to be as we are.

And then Jesus opens his mouth and says, "You must be born again!"

The task is to redeem his words. It is not Oral Roberts or Billy Graham speaking. It is Jesus Christ. The Christ who was born for the sake of the oppressed, who identified with them even unto death, and who initiated his ministry by claiming, as fulfilled in his presence, the prophecy of the Book of Isaiah about preaching good news to the poor, proclaiming release to the captives, and setting at liberty those who are oppressed. It is the long-expected King who commands, "You must be born again."

When evangelists speak of being "born again," they are talking about a religious conversion experience. But Jesus was not talking about a religious experience. He was talking about a change of identity: being born again. Starting all over. Going back to square one. He was talking about a radical identification with those who are blind or hungry or poor, those in bondage and poverty-stricken.

Are we willing to be born again? Are we willing to change our identities? Are we willing to identify with those who have been condemned to second-class citizenship in our society? We resent any restrictions or claims put on our way of life in the name of concern for others. They appear to us as intolerable violations of our individual rights. For us there exists only one right: the right to live in peace and not be disturbed. Like Nicodemus, we want to talk about religion but not politics. We want shortcuts and end up with what Bonhoeffer called "cheap grace." The revival of religion among so-called born-again Christians, is often nothing more than an emotional jag from which believers escape quite unscathed. So our insurance company executive continues his climb to the top: "I want to stay a business-man, but I want people to know that God changes lives."

Unfortunately for him, and for us, the changes demanded by our confrontation with Jesus are eviscerating. They turn us inside out and demand a whole new identity. We are called to make the frustrations of the oppressed our frustrations, their aspirations our aspirations. We are called to make their insecurity our insecurity, their struggle our struggle.

During one evangelistic campaign, posters and bumper stickers were displayed with the slogan, "Jesus is the answer!" On one of the posters someone had penciled in the words, "But what is the question?" Jesus calls into question our comfortable, self-centered, self-affirming identities and calls us to be born again in the image of the crucified one. He is not calling us to be his admirers, much less his defenders. He is calling us to be followers who are willing to take on the scandal of being born in a barn and the embarrassment of an outcast's cross. Black theologian James Cone contends that Christianity is essentially a religion of liberation. Any message that is not related to the liberation of the poor and the oppressed in society is not Christ's message.

But how would we know? If we read the Bible at all, it is usually for our own devotional use rather than any serious study of scripture. For us, Jesus is the one who has the answer. We have the questions. It never occurs to us that he might just call into question our whole being. "You come to me, Nicodemus, as you are, to talk about God, and I say to you, you must be born again. Are you ready to discount your status, your privilege, your success, to identify with the wretched, the lost, and the damned?"

To love God, says Jesus, is to love our neighbor—who, it must be noted, is not the person living next door but any needy person in the world. That covers a lot of uncomfortable ground. But the New Testament writers are adamant. If we cannot love our neighbor, whom we have seen, we cannot love God, whom we have not seen (1 John 4:20). The logic is devastating. John pulls no punches when he says that anyone who claims to love God while hating his brother is a liar. Not uninformed, not short-sighted, not ignorant—a barefaced liar! In most circles, "them's fightin' words."

John's point seems dangerously lacking in the popular spirituality of many Christians in this country. Perhaps there is no characteristic of worldly spirituality that is more at odds with current religious trends than this characteristic of global consciousness and its concern for global good. No longer can we afford the provincialism of "My country, right or wrong." No longer can we grant the assumption that increasing profits for American business is the basic tenet of good economic theory and practice. No longer can we regard national security and economic privilege as sacrosanct.

We may agree that all of this is very idealistic and impractical, not to mention, unpatriotic and inconvenient. But what are we to say to Emmanuel, God with us, born in a barn and hung on a cross? How do we say, "Well, concern for the poverty-plagued Ethiopians is a matter of opinion?" How can I say to Emmanuel that my child's education is more important than that of the kid in the ghetto? God not only is color-blind, but cannot read a map with boundaries dividing the world into sovereign nations.

To call global thinking "idealistic and impractical," is simply to be out of touch with reality. The deterioration of the ozone layer that protects the earth from the ultraviolet rays of sunlight is a global problem, as is the AIDS epidemic and the pollution of oceans. These global problems demand that we think in universal terms. But for us as believers, consideration of the Incarnation will drive us to a global world view, even when nothing else does.

To bear the name of Christ as a "Christian" is to be radically bonded to those who have been overlooked by the distributors of this world's goods and services, those who have been left on the banks of the Besor, those for whom Lady Luck has looked the other way. For us who espouse loyalty to Jesus as Christ and King, sharing God's bounty with those who are too exhausted to compete in the economic olympics is an ethical imperative. Just as with David's macho men, Caesar's law must intervene and create in the chaos a just society. Contemporary spirituality calls us to render to God the things that are Caesar's.

Chapter Six

Religion and Politics Do Mix

Christian spirituality has always been characterized by its loving concern for others. From the days of the early church, when Christians stayed behind the fleeing masses of Roman citizens to care for those who were stricken with the plague—down to the days of marches in Selma or giving sanctuary to Central American refugees—Christians have always been charged with the offense of loving too much.

Traditional spirituality, however, has had trouble seeing the political dimensions of this love. In its focus on heaven, it has approached the ills of this world with emergency ministries. It has had difficulty seeing that the wounds requiring treatment are inflicted by the political and economic structures of society. One denomination official put it, "Local communities, churches, and judicatories have hunger programs that place an inordinate emphasis upon fast days, gleaners' groups, and food distribution programs which emphasize direct food relief, and then frequently ignore the necessity of dealing with systemic change and the fundamental causes of hunger and malnutrition."

A piety that cultivates personal virtues such as love and sensitivity to the needs of others, without addressing the societal causes of human suffering, ill serves its Lord. The gratification of having fought a good fight and remaining true to principles is no substitute for bringing about changes in the system. This is not a time for willing martyrs. It is a time for effective agents of social change. Worldly spirituality forces us to take our love into the political arena where the decisions effecting the system are made.

Most people are of the opinion that politics and religion do not mix, or at least ought not to mix and, consequently, politics is another of those taboo topics in the church. The belief goes back a long way. I imagine the pharaoh of vintage Egypt did not appreciate Moses coming to court with his impudent demand, "Let my people go!" He must have been a firm advocate of the separation of church and state, no doubt because to grant the demand would have disrupted the economy of the nation. Nonetheless, Moses was there because of a holy calling. The commonly held assumption that religion and politics ought not mix, therefore, needs to be examined and, indeed, challenged.

As Americans, we take for granted the guarantees of religious freedom and point with pride to the constitutional provisions that ensure the separation between church and state. But the founding fathers only prohibited the establishment of an official religion, that is, one that enjoys the sponsorship of the state. What the constitution does not prohibit is the mixing of politics and religion as such. For example, we pledge allegiance to the flag and speak of "one nation under God." We print our monetary currency with the affirmation that "in God we trust." Oaths of office are sworn on the Bible. Clearly we do not exclude religion from the political arena.

Furthermore, politics and religion are inevitably mixed in an ideology that could be called "American Civil Religion," but is probably more properly described as "super patriotism." Civil religion endows national self-interest with the aura of divine approval. It is the myth we tell ourselves as Americans about our ultimate significance in the world community of nations.

Historically, the myth was embodied in the pioneer's cry of "manifest destiny." The westward expansion was fueled—nay, justified—by the belief that divine providence had decreed this country should be taken, coast to coast, from the Indians and anyone else who stood in the way. Everything and everyone who got in the path was an obstacle to the divine will. In more recent American history, it was manifested in the Johnson and the Nixon administrations when, convinced we were the saviors of the free world, we sent troops into Vietnam. We saw it in the Carter years when we tried to be the champion of human rights around the world. Most recently we saw it in the Reagan administration when we were told we must be the foremost military power on earth in order to impose our will on others—especially Central Americans—under the guise of stopping "godless Communism."

Every nation brews its own unique brand of civil religion, but each is a heady mixture of patriotic fervor and religious zeal. Under certain conditions, it is capable of making even the most sober citizen drunk with nationalism.

As human beings, we are all religious by nature. Since the beginning of time, we instinctively reach out to something beyond ourselves. We are at least dimly aware that our birth and death are bounded on both sides by the abyss of nothingness. Humbled by the awareness of a life span measured in decades, we feel our individual insignificance and seek to align ourselves with some group, cause, or ideology that transcends our own finiteness and gives it ultimate meaning.

A nation or tribe, on the other hand, has a story or history that sets it apart significantly from all other nations or tribes. Because this story transcends any individual person's limited and relatively insignificant reason for being, it can be transformed into something like religious fervor. Civil religion is the super patriotism that grows out of this primal need for personal significance, a need that the tribe meets with its story of special importance. Civil religion provides both the person and the community with a unique identity, a sense of cosmic destiny.

In Joshua 24—one of the oldest fragments of the oral tradition contained in the Old Testament—the twelve tribes of Israel are pictured as gathering periodically at the sanctuary of Shechem for a covenant renewal ceremony. The liturgy featured, among other activities, the recitation of the events that brought them together as God's people: the call of Abraham, the days of slavery in Egypt, the deliverance from bondage under the leadership of Moses, the years of wandering in the wilderness, and the conquest of the promised land. It was a creedal statement of their divine origin and destiny. It was a reminder to the members of the tribal community that they held a special identity and purpose as God's people. Today's political rallies and conventions echo this ancient tribal activity. The creedal story is recited in speeches and the flags are waved.

Civil religion flourishes in the soil of patriotic willingness to grant ultimate significance to the tribe or nation, as though it carried a sacred calling. "My country 'tis of Thee. . . ," we sing with tears in our eyes and lumps in our throats. The fact that George Bush could make the pledge of allegiance a political issue in the 1988 presidential election, illustrates the emotional—not rational—emotional depth of super patriotism. The same can be said for the feverish response to his presidential proposal that the Constitution be amended to prohibit desecration of the American flag. "Desecration" is a religious term meaning to destroy that which is sacred. Civil religion affirms a nation's flag is holy because it flies over a country that has a divine destiny others do not have, special privileges others do not share, unique responsibilities others do not carry.

The first shots of World War II were fired by Germany, and later joined by Japan, and both of them thought they had a destiny to fulfill by extending their imperial power throughout the world. Britain and the United States returned fire and were energized by the conviction that they were making the world safe for democracy. After its revolution, Russia entered upon a crusade to create a classless society and impose it on the rest of the world. United States foreign policy in Central America has been fueled by the conviction that what is good for the United States is good for the Western hemisphere.

It is because we believe these myths about ourselves and commit ourselves to them with emotional loyalty and energy that religion and politics do mix. And it is for this reason that a worldly spirituality requires that biblical religion and politics must mix. We need a biblical perspective if we are to maintain any sort of critical stance regarding the press releases of vested interests.

When the Bible speaks of the "kingdom" of God it is using political imagery. To proclaim Jesus as "King," "Christ," or "Messiah" is to nominate him in the eyes of the world as a political contender. That is, after all, why the birth of Jesus spooked Herod to infanticide, and popular expectations moved Pilate to impose the death penalty.

The idea that politics and religion do not mix would be foreign, indeed, to biblical writers. Their literary efforts remind us that to be a follower of Christ is to pledge allegiance to a King who is not the head of state or sovereign ruler of the nation in which we dwell. We are to live in the world but not be of it, which makes us aliens in one way or another.

Nearly a half-century of nostalgia has cloaked Dietrich Bonhoeffer in the garb of a Christian martyr and hero of the Faith. But Bonhoeffer, a young Lutheran pastor at the time of World War II, felt he had to break with the National Church of Germany because it was the pawn of German civil religion. It was the mouthpiece of the Third Reich, and its sole purpose was to provide sacred sanction for Hitler's dreams and the policies of the state. At first Bonhoeffer became part of the Confessing Church, which denounced as blasphemous the claims of the National Church. But it stopped short of any overt political action. No doubt, the many good Christians who went to church every Sunday were nourished spiritually, as were the good Christians of Dachau, Bergen-Belsen, and Buchenwald who must have noticed a strange odor in the air on their way to worship. But for Bonhoeffer, traditional spirituality missed the mark. He believed that when a drunken driver is careening down the street killing pedestrians, responsible spirituality requires not only the wounds of the victims be bound, but the driver be stopped. Bonhoeffer became a member of the conspiracy to overthrow the government and assassinate Adolf Hitler. For him Christian spirituality was, in the last analysis, essentially and inescapably political.

Because religion and politics are inevitably mixed in all civil religions, it is crucial that biblical religion and politics be mixed to provide a critical perspective on the claims of the state. Biblical faith reminds us that we are citizens of another kingdom and owe allegiance to a higher power than the reigning administration. As a nation, we have no special claim on God's blessing, no special place in God's eyes. Divine purposes are not tied to our gross national product, the soundness of the dollar, or our national security.

Ancient Israel prided herself on being God's chosen people, but was sold into exile because she assumed the Holy One could not do without her. Always a fatal mistake!

Another reason why politics and biblical religion must mix is because scripture offers a political mandate to the state as well as a critique of its claims. It is to seek the shalom of its constituents.

When Jesus spoke in his hometown synagogue, he began his sermon to the local gentry by quoting the Old Testament Book of Isaiah: "The Spirit of the Lord is upon me, because he has anointed me to preach good news to the poor. He has sent me to proclaim release to the captives and recovering of sight to the blind, to set at liberty those who are oppressed, to proclaim the acceptable year of the Lord" (Luke 4:18, 19). His speech sounds strangely like that of a political candidate running for office, especially since he claimed that the promise was as good as fulfilled by his presence among them. But by doing so, Jesus nailed down one of the central planks in God's political platform.

In both the Old and New Testaments, God is portrayed as the Champion of orphans and widows, the maimed and the sick, captives and aliens. Scripture reveals the divine bias for all those who yearn for a place in the sun and who can never find it. They do not have the necessary clout to balance the vested interests of those who already have a deep tan. To see the world through the eyes of Christ, as we are called to do, we must acknowledge, understand, and accept responsibility for our connectedness to each other in the human family.

Biblical faith demands that religion and politics mix because it sees God's creation as a work of divine love. Law is the political means by which we, in groups, respond to God's creative initiative to love our neighbors and our planet. To love in the way that God has loved us is to work toward a time when the law of the land reflects the divine intention for the world.

There is a crucial distinction to be made between personal acts of love that aim to feed the poor, and political actions that seek to remedy the root causes of poverty. Of course, feeding the poor is required of us, as is offering a cup of water to the thirsty, clothing the naked, and visiting the prisoner. But we live in a world where political systems contribute to an economic stratification in which the rich get richer and the poor get poorer. The lack of educational opportunities, lingering racism, inequality of taxation—all contribute to the complex malaise of poverty. First-aid approaches may salve consciences, but they leave the disease untreated. Love must be spelled out politically and economically if we are to carry out the biblical mandate to love God and our neighbor.

The political groups of which we are unavoidably part make decisions about these people as a whole. These decisions are called "public policy." People live and die because of them. As members of society and citizens of God's kingdom, we have a special obligation to participate actively in making these decisions of public policy.

So far, so good. The problems arise when we quickly discover that we all read the Bible differently. The political imperatives drawn from it in making those policy decisions put us in sharp disagreement. Remember the volleyball game being played in the church league? The ball landed close to the line. All the good Christians on one team were sure the ball landed out-of-bounds while all the good Christians on the other team were just as certain that it landed in-bounds. Both teams were convinced of the correctness of their perception. It was the other team that was mistaken.

The difference between the church and the volleyball game is that there is no referee to make the call. Consequently, the church tends to ignore the close calls. The spiritual consensus has been to leave politics out of all religious discussion. Religion has become a personal thing with the focus on personal virtue and life after death. Life in this world is discussed only in terms of individual ethics, and political views are assumed to be one's own private opinion.

It is precisely this assumption that needs to be challenged. Because politics and religion mix, they must mix in the arena of faith debate, the church. The church does not provide a referee to decide the close calls, but it does offer a place where the close calls can be "cussed and discussed." That is the functional meaning of the church as a priesthood of all believers. To be a priesthood of all believers means more than having a personal hot line to the throne of grace. If anything, it is a party line and always involves the neighbor. When the phone rings, it is a call for each of us to be a priest to one another. As Luther envisioned it, each of us is "to be a Christ to our neighbors," ministering to them out of our best wisdom and understanding of our faith. That is how we grow spiritually.

But we grow in our faith not only through confirmation of it by the company of believers, but by having it challenged and modified through exposure to the views of others. I cannot hold my religious views to myself without robbing my neighbor of the means necessary for his or her development. Since this world is the stage on which God is working to create a kingdom of peace and justice, my political convictions are every bit as important to God and the community of faith as are my religious beliefs. I can, therefore, no more hold my political views to myself than I can my religious convictions. Both my religious and political views are to be shared within the priesthood because either may encourage growth in other believers or be called into question by their rebuttal and require reexamination.

Because the church is not a homogeneous group of people who see things eye-to-eye or who understand God's will in the same way, it will always be a place of lively discussion of diverse views as we try to discover what is God's will. To paraphrase James Gustafson's observation: The church is not a place of religious, much less political, agreement. It is, rather, a place of religious and political discussion in light of scripture. To short-circuit this discussion by quoting a few isolated verses of scripture is not only inadequate, but woefully naive. Scriptural proof-texts cannot be applied to our time as though no water has flowed under the historical bridge.

The issue of drinking, for example, is complicated not only because of the modern technology of distillation, which increases the alcoholic content of beverages, but by the invention of the automobile. In the days of Jesus, a pedestrian had considerable time to get out of the way of a drunken ox-cart driver. Today, travel is vastly different as are the issues involved. They do not lend themselves to the advice of writers for whom speeding automobiles and souped-up horsepower did not exist even in their wildest flights of imagination.

What does it mean to love my neighbor in a labor-management negotiation over wages and working conditions? Who is my neighbor? Is it the person across the bargaining table from me, or is it those whom I represent and to whom I am responsible. What would Jesus do in such a situation? I must confess, I do not know, and neither does anyone else. The Bible never envisioned big business, much less labor unions.

We will, therefore, be left to our own best judgment about the question. We must risk some answer, but it will be a risk of faith, and no doubt other Christians will see the matter differently. We should make our decisions in the best light of our faith at the time and not cop out by compartmentalizing it into worlds of the sacred and the secular, never the twain to meet. We can expect that when politics and religion mix in the arena of faith, as indeed they must, emotions will be ignited and people will get involved. But no one will be bored, a condition sadly present in many churches today. Religious discourse will be heated because it will matter. It will be relevant and carry consequences.

For those who like a biblical precedent for such a model of the church, let me suggest the group of disciples. There, following Jesus along the dusty roads of Galilee, was Matthew, the tax collector. His income was dependent upon retaining the Roman political party in power. He was a company man and voted a straight ticket. There, too, was Simon the Zealot, trudging side-by-side with Matthew on those hot, dusty roads. Like Matthew, he was also a disciple of Jesus. But his political persuasion led him to become a terrorist. Zealots were dedicated to the violent resistance of Roman oppression, including the overthrow of the government. On any normal day—or dark night— Simon would have slipped a knife between the ribs of Matthew the tax collector, and done it to the glory of God! And Matthew would have turned Simon in to the authorities as a revolutionary. Yet there they are. Both of them. Side-by-side. Disciples of Jesus—not because they agreed with one another, but because they were both seeking to be obedient to the calling of discipleship.

What is fascinating is that there is not a shred of evidence to suggest that either of them changed their political views. Assumptions to the contrary bring unwarranted presuppositions to the text. What bound them together was not agreement about religion or politics but that each of them, in his own way, was following Jesus. This meant they had to trust one another's faith and ethics even though they did not agree with either. Imagine the heated arguments they must have had as they walked and talked together! Never a dull moment!

The trouble with most churches today is that there is no evidence of that kind of diversity. Many church leaders, not to mention their constituents, find any difference of opinion, and certainly conflict, to be very threatening. They seek to avoid it at all costs, either by denying it or burying it. Consequently, we have successfully screened out the differences or suppressed them in the name of "peace and unity."

There were at least two Christians in the early church of Rome who were of this mind. They had come to the conclusion that the church was not big enough for both meat eaters and vegetarians (cf. Rom. 14:1–6). Nor was the church big enough for those who gathered to praise God on Sunday and those who believed some other day of the week was just as appropriate for worship. For them, the order of the day seemed to be, "two's company, but three's a crowd!"

The issues, of course, were of great importance in the early church. Each side could make an excellent case. The issue was over the eating of meat offered to idols. It could be bought cheaper in the marketplace, so budget-minded believers contended that since Christ had made them free, it did not matter that the meat had been offered to idols. The vegetarians, on the other hand, said, "No! It is better to abstain. To eat meat offered to an idol is to compromise your witness to the world, and no believer is free to do that."

The argument over which day to worship was equally heated. The Sunday worshipers contended that the first day of the week was the day of resurrection and, consequently, ought to be the day of gathering. Others argued that Christ's resurrection hallowed all of life and, therefore, any day of the week was appropriate for worship. Convenience alone ought to determine the day.

What is startling about Paul's reply to these Roman Christians is that he takes no sides. He offers no opinion about which group is right and which is wrong. Not only does he not judge between the various factions, he insists the church must be large enough to accommodate them all. None is to be excluded. Meat eaters and vegetarians, side-by-side. Sunday worshipers and weekday worshipers, side-by-side. Paul's doctrine of the church is disarmingly simple: "two's company, but three's the church."

The point to be gained is crucial. Christian faith is on trial in the eyes of the world. It looks at the church to see if we put our practice where our proclamation is. Our claim is that God was in Christ reconciling the world. Not merely forgiving it—reconciling it. Forgiveness moves in the direction of the righteous to the sinner and, thereby, maintains in many subtle ways the distinctions and the rifts between them. Reconciliation, on the other hand, is accomplished when equals who differ, nevertheless are able to accept, though not necessarily agree with, each other.

What usually happens in human relations, and certainly in church relations, is not reconciliation in the midst of differences but the elimination of all differences; not conflict managed creatively, but conflict denied. Either churches do not allow conflict, screening out certain practices, people, or beliefs; or they pretend there are no differences and call themselves a fellowship of love simply because disagreements are not taken seriously. In neither case is reconciliation practiced. Because believers are not encouraged to disagree, they do not know what to do with their differences. They become frustrated because they feel their views are not valued. They discover there is no room for them in the community of believers and tend to become bitter because they are not part of the power structure that successfully imposes its will on everyone else. As a result, the differences go underground, where they work as a cancer, sapping the energy of the community of faith, or they erupt in open schism. People who are too different drop out altogether. Or they start another denomination.

The church has to be different from the other organizations of the world. From a Pauline perspective, the problem with a bridge club is that it has no room for the poker players, and the trouble with the Kiwanis club is that it includes no Rotarians. The world is free to set the terms of inclusion for its organizations, but those terms are not to be brought into the church. When the church becomes exclusive, ingrown, and provincial, it becomes merely another elite club—one of the many options offered for folks who already pretty much see eye-to-eye and want a chance to agree with one another. It is not against faith that Paul warns us, it is against "my" faith.

The same can be said for the diversity of political views held by believers. Both the church and the believers in it hold truth in earthen vessels. Neither can afford a messianic complex or a triumphal theology characterized by certainty. We are not able to say with certainty about the kingdom, "Lo, here!" or "At last, there!" Nevertheless, we must risk making some assessments of the ways things are in this world and doing so to the glory of God. "Risk" is the name of the game, and humility and a sense of humor are essential for every player.

"But," you insist, "the church must stand for something. It can't be just a weather vane!"

Right!

But what is the church to stand for? It depends on which Christian you ask. Is worshiping God on Sunday or a weekday the proper time? It depends on whom you poll. The same for the ethics of eating meat or abstaining, pro-choice or pro-life in matters of abortion, labeling homosexuality a "sin" or "a sexual preference" in matters of ordination to the gospel ministry. Articles of faith change. Certainly political assessments do. If the church is to stand for anything, it must be God's reconciling accomplishment in Christ. And for that claim to be credible in the eyes of the world, the evidence must be seen in how the people of God handle their differences. The church is that group of meat eaters and vegetarians, Sunday worshipers and weekday worshipers, Democrats and Republicans who hold their convictions loosely even while attempting to be faithful in their calling as disciples.

The diversity of political perspectives is to be welcomed in the community of faith, but—and this is an important but—as members of the company of believers, we must have our political views challenged by and grounded in the community of faith. Both our religious and political views must be shaped on the anvil of debate within the community of faith, biblical faith. The priesthood of all believers does not offer us the luxury of holding our views privately, but neither does it allow us to hold views simply because we have grown up with them. Nor can we hold them just because it is to our benefit. They must be sterilized by the scalding heat of scripture. Only as we risk speaking out within the community of faith, defending what we believe to be the will of God in light of biblical study and prayer, can we be delivered from bondage to self-interest and the myopia of parochialism.

The unity of the church is not in the oneness of our agreement, but in our common allegiance to Jesus Christ. That which binds us together as a community of faith is our common desire to be obedient to God's will. That which keeps us growing as a priesthood of believers is our difference in understanding the meaning of that obedience.

If the church cannot demonstrate the reconciling power of Christ to the world, it will never be able to convince the world that it has any good news to offer. The world, with all of its pluralism of perspectives and variety of viewpoints, will not be impressed by anything the church has to say as long as it sees simply another group of homogeneous people who enjoy scratching one another's backs. There are plenty of groups for bright bridge-players or happy hymn-singers.

But if the world sees a lively discussion of differences taking place within a fellowship of love, where the discipline of trust carries across the abyss of disagreement, it may take a second look. If the world sees that in Christ there is neither Jew nor Greek, Democrat nor Republican, sees that Word become flesh, it just may be convinced that there is something to this faith that we profess.

The church is more than a political action group. It is a witness to the good news. It is in its very being a model of the Word made flesh. As Bonhoeffer noted, the church is nothing but a section of humanity in which Jesus Christ has really taken form. The church is nothing but a section of pluralistic humanity—meat-eaters and abstainers, liberals and conservatives, Democrats and Republicans—a cross-section of humanity in which the reconciling reality of Christ has taken shape.

Chapter Seven

On Loving Your Enemies

A minister friend of mine was in the habit of telling his little girl a bedtime story each evening before tucking her in for the night. One evening he told her such a thrilling tale her eyes popped open. She sat up in bed studying her father. "Daddy, do you mean it, or are you just preaching?" Sometimes it is hard to know with preachers.

Sometimes it is even hard to know with Jesus. "Love your neighbor," he said. We may have trouble digesting the command but "Love your enemies" positively sticks in our throats. In the political arena, it is important to know who your allies are and who stands with the opposition. Who are your friends and who are your enemies? Worldly Christians want to know: Did he mean it, or was he just preaching?

Unfortunately, he is not here to respond to our interrogation. But we may assume that he was not "just preaching," and meant what he said. After all, in the span of three short years he did manage to acquire enough enemies of sufficient ferocity—political and otherwise—to do him in.

Nevertheless, we have managed to misunderstand him on at least two crucial points. First, we have misunderstood the meaning of love. We think of it as a noun. In our romantic culture, "love" refers to an intense emotion or feeling of affection. When Jesus admonishes us to love our enemies, we hear him demanding that we like them.

Second, we have come to assume that if we manage to become really loving persons, everyone will like us, with the result that we will have no enemies. One of the more popular fantasies nurtured by a pietistic spirituality is that if we could only be more loving people, the world would be a better place. Peace and harmony would break out, and everyone would like us. Being a follower of Christ translates into being a nice guy or gal. The end result is that there is no difference between a friend and an enemy. Not only will love erase the distinction and iron out the differences, but, indeed, we ought not have any enemies. So the pop theology croons, "What the world needs now is love, just love!"

Jesus called his disciples to be lovers. "This I command you, to love one another" (John 15:17). But, always the realist, he immediately warned them,

81

"If the world hates you, know that it has hated me before it hated you. If you were of the world, the world would love its own; but because you are not of the world . . . therefore the world hates you. Remember the word that I said to you, 'A servant is not greater than his master.' If they persecuted me, they will persecute you." (John 15:18–20)

Jesus not only assumed that his followers would have enemies, but that it was important not to confuse the distinction between friends and enemies. Indeed, it is important to identify who our enemies are so that we can love them appropriately, that is, as enemies.

We do not often picture Jesus as angry, much less, violent. Yet there he is in the gospels, overturning the tables of the money-changers—the veins standing out on his neck—driving these opportunistic entrepreneurs out of the Temple with a whip. Jesus loved people. And because he loved them he opposed everything and everybody who tried to take advantage of them.

Shortly after World War II, I visited Berlin. There, standing in the midst of the devastation, were the ruins of the Kaiser Wilhelm Memorial Cathedral. Pockmarked with bullet and shell holes, the great stained glass windows blown out, the steeple broken in two, the place of worship was mute testimony to the ferocity of the street fighting that took place as building by building, block by block the city was taken from the German army. It silently echoed the screams of the dying and the cries of the suffering. I wandered into the bombed-out church. As my eyes became accustomed to the darkness, they could make out a statue still standing in the narthex. It was Jesus with arms outstretched to the city. In the gloom I could see that some vandal had smeared the face with red paint and the robe looked as though it had been splashed with the blood of war. The welcoming Shepherd had been transformed. The expression on the face was a mask of steel-cold fury. The mouth was set, but the eyes seemed to demand of the world: "What have you done?!"

To love people as Jesus did is to stand for something. To stand for justice is to stand against injustice. To stand for truth is to oppose hypocrisy and falsehood. G.K. Chesterton observed that tolerance is the easy virtue of people who do not believe anything. Some unknown bard has put the observation poetically:

Popularity was his middle name.
Its prod was pride, its price was pain.
He never learned the word called, "no."
They spoke of him as "good old Joe."
His life was one long laughing spell,

82

and how he felt you couldn't tell.
His favorite words were, "yes," and "sure."
Yes, good old Joe was Simon Pure.
So when he died they wrote these lines,
and laid him down midst whispering pines.
"Here lies a man—his name was, Joe.
But what he stood for, we'll never know."

"Conflict," is not a dirty word in the vocabulary of worldly spirituality. Love does not mean that we refrain from it or bow to the opposition. Jesus reminded his disciples that if everyone spoke well of them, something was wrong. We need, therefore, to know what and whom to oppose. We cannot pretend as though conflict does not exist. To be a Christian is to love all that Christ loved, and to be the enemy of all that crucified him. To follow him is to make enemies. Jesus did not win a popularity contest. He was awarded a cross, and he bids us take up ours and follow him.

Jesus, the realist, assumes we will have enemies, and it is Jesus, the realist, who bids us love our enemies. Love them, that is, not as friends, but as enemies. Not only does Jesus not want us to erase the distinction between friends and enemies, but he wants us to love enemies in a particular way. Apparently, we need to know who the enemy is so that we can love them as an enemy.

The question immediately arises, "Who dare we call an enemy?"

Most of us make the designation too easily. The label is applied to people we dislike for any one of a number of reasons, most of them quite petty. Sometimes the label is attached to those who disagree with us and challenge our entrenched positions. An old Irish prayer may bring a smile to our face, but it is one of empathetic identification.

May those who love us, love us;
And those that don't love us,
May God turn their hearts;
And if He doesn't turn their hearts,
May He turn their ankles
So we will know them by their limping.

There may be many for whom we would like to offer such a prayer. Happily, God does not demand that we like them, but neither does the Holy One afford us the luxury of calling them enemies. An enemy is not someone we merely dislike or with whom we disagree.

Nor does Jesus permit us to name someone who has wronged us as an enemy. His instructions in this regard are quite clear. We are to forgive the offender seventy times seven. When Jesus cries out through his pain, "Father, forgive them, for they know not what they do," even as they nail him to the cross, he sets a standard of forgiveness in which there is no room for personal grievances. Carrying a grudge has no support in heaven.

Nevertheless, as the old prayer senses, it is important to identify the enemy in some way. But how? Whom may we mark as an enemy?

An enemy is anyone or any institution that opposes the kingdom of God. And the kingdom of God is the Creator's active concern for human well-being establishing itself in history and showering the world with the blessings of shalom. Rather than being part of God's creativity, an enemy is part of the chaos that opposes God's ordering.

In identifying the enemy, the Bible is important. It is God's diary of concern kept by various writers and scribes over the years. The Exodus: a story of God's concern for a slave people and their liberation from oppression. As they slowly learn the lessons of obedience, they become a theocracy; and when they forget to be obedient, the prophets come down from the hills to expose injustice in the courts and marketplace. The greed of the wealthy and the insensitivity of the powerful are denounced.

In the New Testament, Jesus begins his public ministry by linking himself to the messianic promise of the Old Testament, namely, to free the captives, restore sight to the blind, and set at liberty those who are oppressed (Luke 4:18). The gospels portray Jesus as one who "rebukes" (a term of genuine anger) the demons who diminish the health and happiness of the multitudes. At the same time, he feeds the stomachs and spirits of the people, all in the name of abundant life.

Political spirituality dares to discern the signs of the kingdom— those areas in present human history where God's creativity is at work— and name them as such. We may not be able to say, "Lo, here," or "Lo, there," as if we possessed infallible insight. But we must risk saying, "Maybe, here," or "Maybe, there." Then we are to devote ourselves radically to the cultivation of the possibilities.

To make the mountains low, the uneven ground level, and the rough places a plain, however, requires removing obstacles. It requires risking the identification of those obstacles. If we are wrong, God's acceptance of us is greater than our error. If we are right, even though the whole world would oppose us, history will vindicate us. We are liberated from the terror of being wrong and a false humility that is little more than an excuse for not acting. We are freed to name our enemies, which, in turn, frees us to love them.

When Jesus bids us love our enemies, however, he is not talking about liking them. "Love" is not a noun—a feeling or an emotion, as if our ability to respond to his command depended on our endocrine glands. For Jesus, "love," was a verb. It is something we do, whether we feel like it or not. Nowhere is this more clear than when, in speaking of God's love, Jesus points out that God "makes [the] sun rise on the evil and on the good, and sends rain on the just and on the unjust" (Matt. 5:45). Certainly, God does not like the evil or the unjust. Nevertheless, they are the recipients of God's providential actions.

God's love is the current in which history flows. To paddle our canoes with the flow is to experience the current as divine benevolence. To fight the current is to experience the flow as divine wrath. God's love in action is experienced by the oppressed as divine benevolence, while the oppressor feels it as God's wrath.

Consider the events surrounding the Exodus as they might have been reported by an Egyptian eyewitness in the Cairo *Register-Mail.*

The Hebrews? They were a shifty lot. A bunch of drifters, coming in off the desert, not much better than gypsies. They came to us with little culture and less refinement. It's a well known fact that their number included thieves, con-artists, rapists, and murderers—not a very savory group of immigrants. In any case they came here to Egypt, looking for a handout. Which, let it be noted for the record, we gave them. We gave them food, jobs, and a place to stay. To be sure, they weren't the best jobs in the land— day laborers, brickmakers—but, after all beggars can't be choosers. Right?! And they didn't starve. That's the point. They should have been grateful. But, No! They were always complaining. Always wanting something more. And lazy! They seemed more interested in sex and making babies than work. You'd have to say they lacked ambition. Very few of them ever went to school.

And then this outside agitator came in to organize them and deliberately created a disturbance. Everything was nice and peaceful till he showed up, if you know what I mean? They knew their place. But then all hell broke loose. Moses, I think his name was. He had already killed one Egyptian that we know of and came out of hiding somewhere—maybe Libya. Wherever it was, he learned the tactics of terrorism. His only concern was confrontation with government officials. You couldn't reason with him. No talk. Just demands. And that was just the beginning. Next thing we knew he had poisoned our drinking water and food supplies. Deliberate sabotage. I tell you, this Moses was a homicidal maniac. He masterminded a deadly plot to kill us all. There wasn't a household in the entire nation that didn't suffer the loss of someone. It was all part of a plot to destroy our way of life and take over the country. So we deported him and his kind. Good riddance, we thought.

But those grubby, ungrateful troublemakers took everything

they could get their hands on, everything we had given them. They sucked the life blood right out of the economy. Drained the labor pool. Businesses went bankrupt because all the cheap labor was gone. The stock market crashed. Inflation doubled.

Naturally, we tried to rectify the whole situation. We went after them to at least get back our stolen property. But would you believe, our law enforcement officials—who were only doing their duty—were led into an ambush. Their poor wives and children never heard from them again. Those courageous freedom fighters—protecting our country and loved ones, patriotic, God-fearing men, all of them—to a man, wiped out!

The Exodus was a political revolution, though that reality may have escaped our notice in the Sunday school version of the tale. It involved the tactics of intimidation and force. Its results were violence and bloodshed. What is disturbingly clear in the biblical account is: God not only is praised by the Hebrew slaves for their deliverance from bondage, but is credited with being the Mastermind behind the whole plot, including the bloodshed.

Our instinctive inclination is to dismiss such a dreadful bias in the story by claiming, for ourselves, a less bloodthirsty understanding of God, one that pictures God taking little lambs to the divine bosom and gently leading those who are with young. We thereby turn the Lion of Judah into a household pet, tamed and domesticated. Jesus as the messianic King is emasculated as a court eunuch and becomes the private chaplain to tired corporate executives who are exhausted from their efforts to increase profits. "Come to me, all you who labor and are heavy laden, and I will give you rest. . . . Peace, I leave with you. . . ." etc., etc. We have sentimentalized love, just as we have so many of the stories surrounding the King.

The birth narratives of Jesus, and the seasonal sentimentality surrounding them, are a case in point. The birth of King Jesus was a political event with revolutionary implications, and Herod knew it. Matthew's narrative includes the cruel slaying of innocent children (Matt. 2:13–18). And why? Because the power of Herod was threatened. He sensed in this divine visitation something that would challenge Caesar's law and order, alter the priorities of his people, and render relative his authority. Herod was so threatened and enraged that he began a systematic liquidation of all the male children two years of age and under. He was taking no chances. It was perfectly clear to him, if not to us, that Jesus was a subversive.

Talking about the birds of the air and the lilies of the field, healing the sick and blessing the children, Jesus touched a warm and responsive cord in the crowds surrounding his ministry. Great crowds were attracted by his charisma of love and compassion. But almost as if to correct a growing false impression, Jesus uttered these caustic words,

> Do not think that I have come to bring peace on earth; I have not come to bring peace, but a sword. I have come to set a man against his father, and a daughter against her mother, and a daughter-in-law against her mother-in-law; and a man's foes will be those of his own household. He who loves father or mother more than me is not worthy of me; and he who loves son or daughter more than me is not worthy of me. (Matthew 10:34–37)

In light of his obvious concern and compassion, we must wonder where Matthew dug up this quotation. Some scholars have concluded that these alien words were put in Jesus' mouth by Matthew in order to address the situation in the early church. But the sword of division about which Jesus spoke is the inevitable consequence of Christ-like love, and there is no reason to doubt the authenticity of the teaching.

Basic to all of Jesus' teaching was the assertion that all of us have worth in God's eyes—more worth than the lilies of the field, or the birds of the air. The poor, the meek, those who mourn—all are to be blessed. Those who are the outcasts of society, the lepers, the insane, the foreigners, those who have been ignored by the mainstream of life are the ones who have worth in God's sight. He came to love in the name of the Holy One, and that love has set a sword in our midst.

Then the King will say to the people on his left:

> "I was hungry
> and you cut my food stamps,
> took away my school lunch,
> dumped 'surplus' crops like oranges to rot rather than let me eat them.

> "I was thirsty
> and you continued to let the acid rain kill the fish in the lakes,
> and allowed river water to become unfit to drink.

> "I was a stranger without a home
> and you wiped out the subsidies which were my only hope for a decent place to live.

> "I was naked
> and you cut my welfare check so much that I could not buy clothes,
> you wiped out the community service agencies that have been helping me,

the job-training programs that gave me some chance of supporting myself,
the day-care centers which allowed me to work while my children received good care;
you vetoed raising the minimum wage so that I can't afford to work anyway.

"I was sick
and you capped Medicaid so that I was turned away from the hospital.

"I was in prison
and you wiped out the legal services, so that 'equal justice under law' became mockery.
You took away the lawyer helping my family avoid eviction by a condo developer.

"You did all this and more, you said, to save
your economy and balance your budget.
But the money you had been spending to help me you added to your spending for implements of war.

"And you cut the taxes of the affluent so they would have even more while I would have even less."

The American will answer him,
"When did we ever see you hungry or thirsty or a stranger or naked or sick or in prison, and we would not help you?"

The King will reply,
"I tell you, whenever you refused to help one of the least important ones, you refused to help me."[11]

Jesus boils down the obligations of spirituality to just two: We are to love God and love others. But in his eyes these two are, in fact, one and the same. To love the least of these, that is, those who are oppressed, is to love God. Our love of God is measured in terms of justice and therefore, inescapably political. Bonhoeffer was right.

Nevertheless, because we do not like our politics and religion mixed, we do not like to think of God mixed up in the politics of Egypt, much less being responsible for the death of all those Egyptians. Blood on the holy hands runs counter to our idea of a loving God. So we offer various explanations to tame the story. Those were primitive times and their understanding of God was different than ours. We benefit from the teachings and example of Jesus who reveals a God of love, not vengeance.

The problem with our explanation is that it leaves unanswered the question of justice and freedom. Was it right for the Hebrews to resist Egyptian enslavement? Or, did the integrity of personhood justify resistance to the Third Reich? Plucking a more responsive chord: Was the Boston Tea Party and its willful destruction of someone else's property, permissible? Or, in the interest of self-determination, was the American Revolution a morally just cause?

Most Americans would have to answer yes to these questions because to do otherwise would be a denial of our heritage of freedom. Yet, to justify these actions by an appeal to freedom, justice, and human dignity is to say that tyranny in whatever form it expresses itself can, and must, be resisted in the name of some higher authority that ultimately authorizes such resistance.

Resisting is exactly what Moses and the Hebrews did. They resisted the tyranny of oppression in the name of a higher authority: God.

In Jesus, God provides the higher authority that gives all oppressed people permission to live as free people. When Jesus says, "Peace I leave with you; my peace I give to you; not as the world gives do I give to you" (John 14:27), he is not talking to tired, hassled executives who deserve a little rest. On the contrary, he is offering himself as a higher authority to those who labor under the burden of social sin, those who are milked by it, drained by it, used by it. Jesus is telling them that he has come to give them the shalom that the world will not give. Set within the biblical purview of God's concerns, this is a revolutionary invitation to those victimized by society. It is divine permission to lay hold of the shalom that society denies them. It is an open invitation to take it if the world will not share it.

Let us look again, then, at the story of the Exodus. And rather than soften it for Sunday school consumption, let us try to understand it as a political paradigm. Let us see what it tells us about God. Who is this of whom Moses and the prophets speak and whom we see revealed in Jesus?

The first thing that becomes evident in the story is God's clear bias for the underdog. Evenhanded fairness is not the issue for God. God is concerned with political freedom and economic justice for the disenfranchised. Since justice is more likely to be denied to the poor than to the rich, the weak than the powerful, God tips the scales of justice in favor of the slaves. All available resources, including the very forces of the creation are thrown into the balance. The defenseless and disadvantaged discover a divine Advocate in the energy of the universe. The celestial music of the spheres throbs in rhythm to the heartbeat of the widow, the orphan, the slave, the blind, the hungry, the homeless, and the poor.

The second fact that becomes apparent is the appearance of the enemy. Because divine concern rests with those who are oppressed, God's energy moves actively, even ferociously, in the direction of freedom. It seeks to give the slaves their place in the sun. The inertia of the status quo resists the necessary changes. Consequently, the Egyptian political, economic, and finally the military powers, must be dismantled so that justice can emerge. As God's active concern for human well-being is activated in the lives of people, the enemy emerges. We do not have to make enemies, they appear uninvited! Pick up any newspaper and put on the spectacles of faith. Wherever the oppressed, the diseased, the poverty-stricken, the powerless are being freed from their bondage, there the Creator God is at work. And there, too, will be the enemy opposing the Creator's efforts—the privileged pharaohs of the world who champion the status quo, resist change, and try to hold on to what they have.

The third lesson to be learned from the story is that God plays hard ball. You do not mess around with God. God is more interested in freedom for slaves than in the fatness of their owners' pocketbooks. God is more interested in freedom of residence than in maintaining property values in the suburbs. We cannot read the story and miss the point that those who try to maintain an advantageous status quo at the expense of others will not be able to escape forever the judgment of history. Those who try to hold the lid of repression on anyone in the name of an expanding economy, loyalty to country, or respect for law and order will feel the wrath of the Lion of Judah.

Because God means business, love of an enemy differs from the love of a friend in at least two respects. First, an enemy stands in God's way and, therefore, needs to be warned. An enemy is in danger of being the target of God's wrath. Our love of enemies requires identification of them and then alerting them to their precarious situation. God's love, as the pharaoh found out, can pulverize the opposition. To love the enemies when they are in the way of God's kingdom is to warn them that they are standing directly in the path of God's liberating bulldozer. For their own good they need to move out of the way by ceasing to operate as an oppressor or be ground into the dust of history. As the exasperated Quaker farmer said to his obstreperous cow who had kicked over the milk bucket for the third time, "Thou knowest I would not hurt thee for anything in the world, but thou art standing right where I am about to shoot!"

I take it that one of the functions of preaching and Bible study in the church is to declare the risks involved to the enemy. It is another side of proclamation. Let us be clear, however, that the judgment being proclaimed has little to do with traditional spirituality that emphasizes the individual soul standing before God on the last day. It is, rather, a political statement about justice.

The second way in which love of enemies differs from love of friends is that it denies them their power to define the terms of human existence. To love the oppressor as a child of God is to set that person in the context of God's kingdom of liberation. In that kingdom the enemy is denied his or her right to be an oppressor.

Jesus uses the example of turning the other cheek. To do so denies the enemy's right to set the terms of the relationship. By turning the other cheek, the "victim" has taken control of the situation and creates a new reality. It is the reality of two equals. To be sure, turning the other cheek is a nonviolent way of demonstrating liberation from oppression, but it is not the only way of doing so and cannot be given legalistic status. Jesus was not setting forth a code of nonviolent conduct. Rather, he was demonstrating an attitude with regard to those who assume they have the right to set the terms of existence and the power to define others as "victims."

But what about violence? Does God not love all people? Yes, of course. But God loves all of us as we are, that is, as sinners. Reality, as well as religion, argues that all people tend to be selfish and hypocritical. Nevertheless, individual human beings have the capacity to love one another. Groups of persons, on the other hand, do not. They are social entities and, unlike human beings, cannot love or hate. Republicans can love. Democrats can love. But neither the Republican nor the Democratic party can love. Nor can General Motors or the United Auto Workers. They can only make collective decisions that seek a just social structure for their constituents. This means the most that can be hoped for in a society of sinners is a dynamic tension between self-interest groups of equal power.

The problem, of course, comes when privileged people are asked to give up some of their power voluntarily for the sake of a more equitable balance. The record indicates they will not. Some kind of coercion becomes necessary in order to deny the powerful their assumed right to retain their privileged position. Once we see that coercion is necessary as an expression of love for all people, the issue of violent or nonviolent coercion is a question of kind, not principle.

As Christians, we would always opt for nonviolent coercion. But whether it remains nonviolent or becomes violent—due to the desperate frustration of the oppressed—depends upon how tightly those with the power, grasp the throats of their victims. If the pharaoh's advisers had been able to convince him which way the current of history was moving, there would have been no plagues and no violence. But the pharaoh's heart was hardened. He would not relinquish any of his power or privilege. Consequently, God, who loves freedom and dignity for all people, moved in. The divine love was experienced by the Hebrews as grace. Egypt experienced it as holy wrath.

> Thus the LORD saved Israel that day from the hand of the Egyptians; and Israel saw the Egyptians dead upon the seashore. And Israel saw the great work which the LORD did against the Egyptians, and the people feared the LORD; and they believed in the Lord . . . (Exodus 14:30, 31)

Spirituality for this world affirms the absolute sovereignty of God over the whole of creation. This means that ultimate allegiance belongs only to God, Caesar notwithstanding. As believers, we must learn not to wince at the thought of civil disobedience when the law and order of Caesar violate God's creative ordering of the world.

The golden thread of Christian civil disobedience in this country goes back a long way, beginning with the signing of the Declaration of Independence. Among those who took up the pen was a Presbyterian minister, John Witherspoon. The golden courage that he and the other signers exhibited by defying the crown has been polished by the passage of time and woven into the fabric of our national memory.

More recently, the lunch counter sit-ins and draft card burnings of the sixties, the refusal to pay taxes and offering sanctuary to illegal aliens in the eighties—though as yet less cherished in our collective consciousness—have contributed to the conscience of the nation. Understandably, the wounds of corrective surgery on the body politic heal slowly and may remain tender to our probing for some time. But these more recent patterns of civil disobedience must also be seen as part of the fabric in our country's tapestry of values and ideals.

Though always controversial by their very nature, acts of civil disobedience have always appealed to a higher authority. By so doing, those who have carried them out remind the rest of us who claim Christ as Lord that our ultimate allegiance lies elsewhere. Worldly spirituality obligates us, by a freedom rooted in the Bible, to deny sovereignty to all laws that contradict human dignity. Through such disobedience to the state, the disciple affirms an allegiance to a higher authority. It is called the kingdom of God.

Chapter Eight

Living the Alternatives

When the church celebrates Palm Sunday, it affirms a tradition with political ramifications as old as the gospel narratives themselves. The story of the triumphal entry into Jerusalem is told by all four of the gospel writers and portrays Jesus meeting the powers of this world head on—taking on those who define reality, politically, economically, religiously—in a showdown. And when it was over and the dust had settled, the resurrection story claimed: Those powers had been dismantled.

The universal question with which spirituality has wrestled in every generation of believers since the days of the early church is: "How do you confess Jesus as your king when this guy in Rome thinks he's the emperor?"

The dean of television newscasters, Walter Cronkite, used to conclude his summary of the evening news by saying, "And that's the way it is. . . ." Political, industrial, and religious bureaucrats echo the words, and usually add, "Take it or leave it!" The definers of worldly reality assume they have the right to say how it is and how it will be. They know who sets the terms. They know who is in charge, and everyone else had better know it, too, because that is the way it is.

For a person who is terminally ill, the all-knowing (though not all-powerful) doctor defines reality. For those of us who live this side of death, any hint of it, such as serious illness or financial reversal, tends to have overwhelming power to depress us and shut us off from life. The employers of the business world define reality for others. They are the ones who set the terms of life and death, success and failure. They determine our worth by putting a price on our services. They set the rules. We either shape up or are shipped out. And when we go, our sense of worth goes too. Unless, of course, we happen to buy the Jesus story. Because, if we do, the gospel newscasters are telling us, "No, that's not the way it is at all! There was this showdown in Jerusalem. Jesus is the boss, and that's the way it is."

The question before the house is: "Do we believe them?"

To believe is not simply to affirm certain doctrinal statements of faith. To believe in Jesus as Lord is to refuse to acknowledge anyone else as king. It is to insist that the powers of this world do not have authority over us, even when they appear to be in charge.

A Russian diplomat residing in this country and discovered to be a spy serves to illustrate this aspect of our faith. In this case, the diplomat was a man with a mission. His values, loyalties, and sense of purpose were all in accord with his government's best interests and not determined by the standards of this country. His citizenship belonged elsewhere. Our government, therefore, correctly saw his presence in the United States as subversive. Similarly, the New Testament calls us to be ambassadors for Christ, living in this world, but not of it. We are not to reject this world, but to live in it—live in it as those who know we are here on a mission. We serve in a diplomatic capacity, representing a kingdom that claims our allegiance. The risk, of course, is that we will be perceived as subversives by a world into which we refuse to fit. But that is the risk we are called to take by a spirituality that takes this world seriously.

Christian spirituality is not only worldly, but also essentially countercultural. The subversive significance in that creedal recitation of the Old Testament tribal gathering at Shechem is often overlooked. "Choose this day whom you will serve, whether the gods your fathers served in the region beyond the River, or the gods of the Amorites in whose land you dwell; but as for me and my house, we will serve the LORD" (Joshua 24:15). The decision whether to serve the well-established gods of the surrounding culture or the God of Exodus and deliverance was a call to be an alternative community. It is quite clear that in affirming their mythic story the tribes were stating their identity as Yahweh's people. Their faith story and the identity that it conveyed to them was clearly countercultural. Joshua and the twelve tribes of Israel were choosing a different God and an alternative set of social values. The function of this annual gathering at Shechem was to affirm and maintain a citizenship different from that of the land in which they resided.

To affirm our citizenship in the kingdom is to live as though the powers of this world have no final claim on us. They do not own us nor do they define our identity. The gospel call to repentance is appropriate, not as a confession of our sins but to assert new loyalties. Jesus declares a new reality and challenges the assumptions of a *quid pro quo* world. To those who think that all the categories of life are fixed and the world is a closed system in which there are no surprises, the gospel comes as good news. Faith in Christ brings unexpected alternatives into such an unimaginative world.

Consider, for example, the story of Zacchaeus, the despised tax collector who made his living by cheating everyone. When Jesus came to town, Zacchaeus, being very short of stature, decided to climb a tree for a better look. Jesus noticed him out on his limb but the question was, What should he, as Messiah, do? Try to change Zacchaeus? The townspeople would have insisted, "You might as well try to turn stones into bread." Those things just do not happen. The options, therefore, were quite clear:

(a) Scold Zacchaeus for being a sinner.

(b) Ignore Zacchaeus because to recognize him in any way gives tacit support to his dishonest dealings.

(c) Laugh at Zacchaeus. He is, after all, a ridiculous spectacle—up a tree.

But Jesus selects a forgotten option:

(d) None of the above. He asks Zacchaeus to come down from the tree and invites himself to Zacchaeus' house for dinner and conversation. And the next day the story is flying around town: "Zacchaeus is a changed man. He's not only giving back what he's stolen, but he's giving it back four times over!"

One of the most certain indicators of Jesus' divinity is not his virgin birth nor his ability to perform miracles. The surest sign that this Jesus is the "Son of the Most High God"/ is his *modus operandi*, his style. He lives the forgotten alternative.

When faced with the dilemma of five thousand hungry people late in the day, his disciples came to him with the question, "What shall we do?" Worldly wisdom would suggest:

(a) Tell them to go home.

(b) Tell them to go hungry.

(c) Tell them to get a bite at McDonalds and reconvene at eight o'clock.

Jesus said, "There's another option:

(d) None of the above.

We will bless what we have and feed them now. We will work with what we have and multiply it."

Christ gives us permission to look at the world differently and thereby frees us from the claims and definitions of the reigning authorities. Life is not settled. The way we have been told it is not the way it is at all. The espousers of liberation theology have correctly seen that to take the Jesus story seriously, that is, to have faith in Christ, is to receive permission to play the game by different rules than those set by the protectors of privilege. It is to espouse different values than those held by the brokers of wealth and power.

In a technological society, where everything is explained by a cause-and-effect world view, the options of possibility are seen as limited and become predictable. Herbert Marcuse argues that our Western obsession with practicality has narrowed the limits of life until there are no choices left us than to be practical. What works is good. The end justifies the means. As a result, the ability to criticize our society is slowly being taken from us, and we will no longer be able to conceive of other ways to do things. Faith in Christ offers us the necessary alternatives.

If I have any criticism of the feminist movement, it is its use of the term "liberation." The movement toward women's liberation is really a movement toward women's equality. It is motivated by a concern to provide women an equal chance to get into the courts where the power games are played, an equal chance to set up the tables of the money changers, an equal chance to define the realities of a *quid pro quo* world. But that is not liberation. That is no alternative. That is simply an equal chance for women to have their share of the heart attacks and ulcers. Real liberation comes when people deny credibility to the reigning value system. Only then are true alternatives opened.

The Jesus story opens such alternatives for us. That is why it, and the other stories in the Bible, are important for our spirituality. We live by the stories we tell ourselves. They shape our perceptions of reality. The church, as a story-telling community, creates a special perception of self and the world in which we, as believers, live. Old Testament Israel saw herself as a chosen nation—the "called" people of God— while the New Testament church spoke of itself as a "royal priesthood." Today, the worshiping community must offer an alternative identity to those of us trying to live in the world while not being of it.

It is essential that the company of believers derive this identity from its storybook, the Bible. After all, if you are going to be a member of the McClelland family, let us say, you tell McClelland stories, not Johnson stories: Daddy Mac's rags to riches odyssey, Christie's miracle birth, the skeletons in Cousin Edith's closet, and on and on. It is a matter of cultural conditioning. Not that there is anything wrong with Johnson stories. It is just that they are not crucial to being a McClelland.

The Bible has always been an important part of Christian spirituality because it is, as it were, the family scrapbook. The Bible is that collection of stories and faith statements that the family of God has found to be important in maintaining its distinctive identity over the years. It serves as an important reminder of who we are. When my son, Steven, left home for his first year of college, his mother and I said "Goodbye" to him and admonished, "Remember you are a McClelland." By so doing we were hoping he would recall the family stories that gave his name meaning, hoping he would reaffirm the tradition of integrity that had been given to him by his ancestors who carried the name before him. In his new environment, away from home, we wanted him to remember where his identity was rooted.

During the dark days of slavery in this country, many uprooted Africans retained their identity as a countercultural community by remembering who they were. Long before Jesse Jackson, black preachers were telling their slave congregations "black is beautiful." Long before Rosa Parks, black "mammies" were telling Bible stories, reminding their children they were children of God, not property to be bought and sold. The victory of blacks was their stubborn refusal to let the institution of slavery define them. They denied its power at the heart of their identity.

Similarly, we need to rehearse again and again, and yet again, the stories that give us our identity as God's people. They free us from the myths and claims of the world about who has the power and how reality is to be understood. It is this book, the Bible, that traces the thread of divine dealings with our world and its inhabitants and provides us with the story line in which we see ourselves reflected; characters in an ongoing drama. The purpose of the church's story telling, both in its educational and liturgical role, is to enable its constituency to try out, imaginatively, other options than the scripts written and prescribed by society. The narratives and faith statements of our storybook do not necessarily answer our questions nor solve our problems, but they do enable us to identify with its characters and live with their perspective on life before us. They offer alternative grounds for hope than those the world provides.

In story after story the alternative catches us by surprise. Turn again to the account of the Exodus, that story about an enslaved people held in bondage by the oppressive economic system of the Egyptians. What grounds for hope do they have? Coventional religious wisdom might have suggested putting faith in:

(a) A God who advocates law and order and believes that differences should be negotiated, taken to the courts, and settled through the legal channels provided for settling disputes.

(b) A God who rewards hard work and frowns upon laziness, assuring those who want to get ahead that they can climb the ladder of success by exerting themselves and applying themselves diligently to their work.

(c) A God of peace, who calls us to be content with our lot in life and bids us fit the yoke of spiritual discipline to our necks in order to learn the hard lessons of patience and humility.

(d) None of the above.

The Bible again makes it clear that (d) is the correct answer. God is not to be understood in any of the above categories. The Lion of Judah is a God who champions the cause of marginalized people and who will fight on their behalf. Far from being impartial, Yahweh is an advocate for their cause even espousing violence and bloodshed.

Often these Bible stories are read and dismissed in the same way we read children's fairy tales, "Once upon a time . . . and they all lived happily ever after."

But to examine these stories in light of the familiar worldly wisdom contained in options (a), (b), and (c), and then to discover the alternative possibility, (d) None of the above, is to see that these stories display a radically creative approach to life. They are more illustrative of a view of life than miraculous happenings. They are stories that refuse to accept the established categories of life as fixed. They are counter-cultural. A response to life that says, "None of the above," is a response which sees that the options offered do not fit.

When Jesus insisted, "My kingdom is not of this world," we assumed he was talking about heaven. But to look at these Bible stories from the perspective of worldly spirituality is to discover a radically imaginative approach to this life. The categories of this world are not finally settled. The definitions that fetter us are not forged in steel. Jesus and the gospel writers look at life from a different and radically imaginative perspective and therein lies the kingdom of God. They invite us to live by faith in a God who consistently offers another option than those seen by the authorities and power brokers of this world. An option that fits "None of the above."

So Jesus comes to the poor. The poor, who have long since learned that they have been born poor, they are poor, and they will die poor. Society has defined their possibilities as nil. But Jesus says, "None of the above. Blessed are the poor." And to the meek who know their place in the social pecking order, Jesus turns their understanding of life on its ear by declaring, "Blessed are the meek, for they shall inherit the earth" (Matt. 5:5).

To the rich who know what and whom they can buy and sell, who gather for cocktails at the country club while they benefit from the work of others, those who have life under control and know how much is in their pension fund so they can make secure plans for their retirement, Jesus levels the blockbuster, "It will be more difficult for you to make it into the kingdom of heaven than for a camel to get through a needle's eye!" (cf. Matt. 19:24).

It was not a halo around his head nor a bag of tricks under his toga that caused such a commotion among the authorities. It was the way he looked at life. "There's nothing settled about it!" he insisted. "We don't have to grant as final, the present situation." Jesus is the Son of God and our Savior because he gives us permission to be in this world but not of it, not defined by its options, not bound by its alternatives. Therein lies his subversiveness.

Our faith offers us a different story. It contrasts sharply with the old tune that insists what is good for General Motors—or our national security—is good for the world. It provides us with new spectacles for viewing our situation. With them we see clearly a world pregnant with possibilities. Therein lies its subversiveness.

Ours is worldly faith. Jesus was not crucified in a cathedral between two candles, but on a cross between two criminals, on the town garbage heap, at a crossroads so cosmopolitan that they had to write the charge against him in three languages, at the kind of place where cynics talk smut, and thieves curse, and soldiers gamble. Because that is where he died and what he died about, that is where Christians should be and what Christians should be about. And therein lies our subversiveness.

It is important for the family of faith to tell its stories in such a way that they free us from the propaganda of vested interests. They offer a different view of church and society, which we can affirm as citizens of God's kingdom. It is a Kingdom not of this world and consequently able to bring life where this world sees only death. These stories proclaim a king who offers freedom. We are no longer victims who have no options other than those stated by the rulers of this world. Christ expands our possibilities by giving us permission to shout and cheer where worldly authorities say, "Tell your disciples to keep quiet!" (cf. Luke 19:39). He invites us to dance and sing in a world of despair that declares, "This is the end! Be depressed!"

To adopt such a different view may mean crucifixion at the hands of Caesar. But the resurrection discloses the relativity of earthly power and the nature of God's. It is simply a word that challenges principalities and dares to declare openly the emperor is stark naked—and as vulnerable as the rest of us.

St. Louis or New York or Podunk Center are the Jerusalems in which the alternative must be risked, day after day, week after week. It is in the kingdoms of this world that the definers of reality claim their power and authority to own and rule. But we take the dare because the Jesus story tells us that once there was this showdown in Jerusalem that blew these very powers off their thrones.

So, returning to the question, "Do we believe it?"

Christian spirituality continually raises the question for us. And probably the answer is, when we are completely honest, "Well, yes; but . . . ." So, we, like the disciples before us, cry out, "Lord, increase our faith!" We are fully aware that we need more faith. We have some but it is not nearly enough. Like money, we would like to have more of it. Saints have more faith than doubters or sinners, and clearly we want to be on the side of the angels.

Furthermore, we assume, as did the disciples, that Jesus is the one to see about increasing our store of faith. They came to Jesus with the request. So do we.

His reply to them, as it probably would be to us, is, "If you had faith as a grain of mustard seed, you could say to this sycamine tree,

'Be rooted up, and be planted in the sea,' and it would obey you" (Luke 17:6).

Jesus offers what appears to be a smart-aleck answer. "If you had faith as a grain of mustard seed, you could tell that sycamore tree to move over, and it would do it. If you had even a little faith you could move mountains." In the eyes of Jesus, the disciples apparently had no faith whatsoever! None! Zip! Even a little of it can work wonders, but Jesus says they have not as much as a grain of mustard seed. Evidence: The trees remain rooted.

Can anyone take Jesus seriously? Does any believer truly think that if he or she had enough faith, mountains could be coaxed into leaping around like lambs or trees taken for a stroll? I put it to you that even the most spiritual, deeply committed Christian is doomed to despair if we take the words of Jesus literally. "If between you guys there was enough faith to fill a mustard seed—even that much faith— you could change the landscape," he tells the disciples. Clearly, his reply is at the very least insensitive to their request, not to mention our soul's sincere desire. And at worst, it exhibits callous cynicism.

But Jesus is not one to offer smart-aleck answers. That is not his style. He is not trying to put his disciples down or make us feel stupid. Rather, he is cutting off at the pass our assumptions about faith.

His reply makes it clear that faith does not have to do with God, heaven, or anything else spiritual. On the contrary, faith changes the landscape of this world. It moves mountains and transplants trees. It is not a passport to heaven nor is it a belief about God. Faith is not even belief in God. It is a new understanding of the way this world can be. Faith is an alternative vision of how things can be. It sees with amazing clarity a reality that others do not yet see. It sees the divine alternative.

It is said that the great Michelangelo attracted a crowd of spectators as he worked. One child in particular was fascinated by the sight of chips flying and the sound of mallet on chisel as the master shaped a large block of white marble. Unable to contain her curiosity, she inquired, "What are you making?" Pausing, he replied, "There is an angel in there and I must set it free."

Faith is seeing the new reality and working to set it free. It is seeing the reality of God's kingdom and working with the Holy One to create the new heaven and earth.

To those who have spiritualized faith by insisting that it has to do with things otherworldly, these words of Jesus come as a shock. Faith has to do with this world and seeing it in a different way. There is mounting evidence in the field of cancer research, for example, that faith healing has little to do with belief in God. The research data suggest that patients who are terminally ill, and for whom there is no known cure, have a statistically significant chance of getting well if they can imagine the white blood cells as a victorious army putting to rout the invading army of cancer cells. Faith in divine providence is not necessary. Indeed, faith healing may well be simply a matter of mentally imaging the body as healthy. Recovery is determined, not by faith in God, but by the ability to imagine ourselves as well. Faith in this sense is imaginative vision that sees what medical science and others are not yet able to see.

To visualize that which is not, is a uniquely human possibility. Human responsibility—stewardship, if you will—for our planet and our individual lives rests on our capacity for envisioning alternative possibilities to existing realities. That is why it is crucial to be intentional about what we visualize. We are always imagining a future of some sort and letting our lives be shaped by the vision. Faith seeks to fulfill its own prophecy. If we believe that we can be well, our bodies begin to shape themselves around the new vision of health. If we believe that nuclear suicide is inevitable, we, and our government, begin consciously or unconsciously, to speed up the process. Faith is simply living as though this is true or that is possible. The object of faith may be a variable, but faith itself, is a unique attribute indigenous to the human enterprise. Faith, in the sense that Jesus spoke of it with his disciples, is simply envisioning and practicing an alternative future. It is daring to risk living by a new vision.

Fortunately, according to Jesus, it does not take much faith to shape the world. Even a little vision of new possibilities, as small as a grain of mustard, can work wonders. It can uproot trees, transplant mountains, or disarm a nuclear missile in its launch silo. The quantity of faith is not the issue. Apparently a person either has faith-vision or does not. We either live in a world of possibilities or we live in a world of inevitabilities.

The world has gone about its entrenched ways for a long time, and injustice proves to be a stubborn resistor to change. Neither yields readily without patient pressure. As a result, the wrongs are not redressed and grievances are not corrected. We become impatient, then cynical, and finally self-centered. We put shutters on the windows of our minds to block out the ugly sights and turn in on ourselves, contemplating our navels through body building, dieting, and meditation. We come home from work to play with the kids, watch football on TV, work on the house and yard, and put up a privacy fence to keep the world out. We support preachers and politicians that espouse "family" values. Nothing else seems possible.

One of the difficulties we encounter in trying to deal with the issues facing our country and the world—unemployment, poverty, human and civil rights, and disarmament, to name only a few—is the paralysis that grips our society. We are overwhelmed and, therefore, immobilized by the magnitude of the issues. The public feels powerless. As a result, politicians can play on our lethargy and get by with clichés, easy answers, empty promises, and trite solutions. "The issues are too complex," we are told, so we let the "experts" deal with them. But the "experts" frequently do not deal with them, and confidence in government "of the people and for the people" has been eroded.

In the face of such hopelessness, spirituality must call for a miracle of faith. Nothing else can save us. Nothing else can break the bonds of fear and futility. It does not have to be much faith, says Jesus, but it does have to be new. Faith is a new vision.

If mainline churches are languishing today, perhaps it is because we have no vision that grips the imagination, none compelling enough to command our allegiance and demand our best energies. The Old Testament prophets proclaimed the word of the Lord with the wind in their beards and fire in their eyes, convinced that, without a vision, the people would perish.

When Ezekiel sat in the valley of dried bones contemplating the future of his people, he saw no hope. It was as if the Jewish people had been scattered like so many bleached bones lying in the sun. They were not only dead, but scattered. The situation was quite hopeless. In precisely that unlikely cradle, faith was born. The word of the Lord came to Ezekiel, bringing with it a new vision of the possible. "Behold," God declared, "I will cause breath to enter these bones and they shall live. They shall be joined together and stand before me." In the face of such a vision, his feelings of inadequacy and powerlessness were luxuries Ezekiel simply could not afford (cf. Ezekiel 37).

To be made to feel powerless is a satanic trick. We have been duped by a bad story if we feel helpless. The Jesus story makes it clear that any alternative vision can reshape the world, even if it is as small as a grain of mustard seed. The way to crumble the concrete highway, which our world sweeps down with suicidal speed, is to plant a seed of an alternative vision right beside it. In time, the seed will sprout and grow into a mighty tree; its roots reaching and expanding under the road. Eventually the cement will crack and give way to the vitality of life.

The promise of life in that tiny seed is our hope. It is also a threat because its vitality challenges the powers of death. Faith's vision is destructive as well as creative. There is a dark side to it. It may be compelling, but it is also frightening. It calls on reserves of imagination that see beyond what is. It threatens to disrupt the status quo. Instinctively we know that the comfort and security of our vested interests are in jeopardy. So we try to ignore it, discredit it, or destroy it. Jesus was crucified not only as a political threat to the Roman empire, but as a spiritual threat to the religious establishment. Dead, the religious leaders could say what they wanted to about him. Alive, he spoke for himself! Therein lies the danger of a vision. It is like a live grenade rolling around among the troops. You never know when it will go off in someone's imagination.

The words of Jesus have survived the years not only because they enjoy the benefits of divine inspiration but because their imagery has had the power to grip the imagination. This is especially true of his parables. Here is a noncanonical parable which, while laying no claim to divine inspiration, may yet spark our imagination.

Once a farmer sought to raise a single baby eagle which he had found in the wilderness. He raised it with his chickens and it grew strong. But alas! this king of birds came to think of itself as a chicken rather than an eagle. Each day the farmer would throw it into the air hoping to see it fly, and each time it would return to the earth to eat the chicken feed thrown on the ground. One day, however, something began to stir in the bird's memory when it was launched aloft. A strange and fearful excitement surged through its breast. It stretched its wings and soared, lifted by the rising currents of air. The farmer was ecstatic—until the eagle, sensing its true nature, swooped down on the chickens scratching in the barnyard, and devoured them.

The Jesus story has such carnivorous capabilities because it grips the imagination and calls forth a vision of new possibilities that can destroy the old. Yet, it is the hope of the world. For believers living in, but not of, this world, faith in Christ may or may not have anything to do with life eternal, but it clearly has to do with this life. In him we see, with the eyes of faith, God's vision of the kingdom of God. We begin to think in alternative terms and dare to live in a new reality; a new heaven and a new earth.

Chapter Nine

Called to Be Carnal

So far, the ethical imperative called for by a worldly spirituality has been the distribution of shalom blessings through financial and political means. But the body, too, can be an appropriate instrument for receiving and sharing shalom. Consequently, while dancing may not be an ethical imperative, time and again, the Bible speaks of it as an entirely natural bodily response to the joy of the Lord. The psalmist writes of coming into the Temple for worship, with trimbrel and dance, (Psalm 150:4); and Jesus tells of the dancing that characterized the celebration of the prodigal's return to the father's house of plenty (Luke 15:25). Dancing seems to be an instinctive reaction of the body to the bounteous blessings of God.

Yet, Jesus observed that we are often like people for whom God has piped but who refuse to dance (Luke 7:32). We come to the ball but, like wallflowers, we stand on the sidelines, watching others have the fun.

I suspect our reluctance is not because we are unappreciative of God's generosity so much as because we fear clumsiness and feel self-consciousness. We are afraid to live in our bodies, and frequently resent those who do. Living in them offends our sense of spiritual decorum. Significantly, when David danced before the Lord (2 Sam. 6:14-21), he was despised by his wife, Michal.

Unfortunately, Michal is ever present. The dualistic bias that jaundiced the eyes of the church with regard to the world of finances and politics has also infected with skepticism its view of the bodies with which we must dance in the physical world.

Believers often attend church only to be warned, and sometimes scolded, about the temptations of this life rather than invited to live and celebrate it as a divine gift. Prayers, hymns, and sermons make much of the fact that we are sinners and seem to assume we have much to confess. Moreover, the locus of worldly sin and temptation has typically become focused on our sexuality. Many Christians assume that the so-called unforgivable sin has something to do with sex, and they are convinced that, whatever it is, they have committed it. Religious beliefs have too often focused on human depravity rather than human dignity and have fostered an individualistic, introspective approach to faith that has given human nature, and especially our sexual nature, a bad name.

We must not forget that the Bible has something far more important to focus on than our peccadilloes; sexual or otherwise. It claims that we are created in the image of God. Though we may indeed have feet of clay we are, in God's eyes, at least, ranked only slightly lower on the divine scale than the Holy One (cf. Psalm 8:5). And the foundation of our faith rests on the joyous good news of the Incarnation.

At the root of our word "incarnation" is the word, "carnal," which the dictionary defines: "In or of the flesh; bodily; material or worldly, not spiritual; having to do with or preoccupied with bodily or sexual pleasures; sensual or sexual." The story of Incarnation demands our reflection on the shocking realization that the Most High is preoccupied with bodily, sensual, or sexual pleasures, not spiritual. When God decided to reveal the true nature of divinity, the Holy One did so in a body. God came as a sexual creature. God came carnally.

The church has always had trouble accepting that fact. In the early creeds of the church, for example, God was spoken of as having no "body, parts, or passions." It was offensive to think of a Supreme Being in those terms. Theologians have been embarrassed by the frank anthropomorphism of the Old Testament storytellers, who speak of God's using a body to walk in the garden (Gen. 3:8), smelling the incense (Gen. 8:21), and looking at rainbows (Gen. 9:16).

The early church was influenced by two significant factors that determined its understanding of God's divinity. The first was the reaction of the Greco-Roman empire to the proclamation of the gospel. Although some of its inhabitants became converts, the basic response was one of rejection and persecution. At first only Judaism was offended, then threatened, by the proclamation of Jesus as Messiah. Later, though more for political reasons than religious, the Roman authorities were threatened. What was being proclaimed was a new thing. Christian preachers were saying that the old wineskins of the Jewish Torah were not adequate to contain the freedom that faith in Christ as Lord and Savior afforded. Roman demands for allegiance to, and worship of, the emperor were incompatible with the vision of God's kingdom and obedience to the divine will. Both the religious and social worlds in which the church found itself reacted negatively to its message. The hostility was expressed in occasional outbursts of violence. But even when the persecution was not overt, the threat of its eruption was ever present. The experience of the church led it to the theological conclusion that the world was antagonistic to the gospel. Therefore, the world must be an evil empire, under the influence of a demonic power that sought to erase Christian faith from the scene.

The other factor that influenced the church's theological development was, as we have noted earlier, the dualistic philosophy of the Greco-Roman world. The material or historical world was seen as inferior when compared to the nonphysical realm of the mind and/or spirit.

With a dualistic world view in mind and the threat of persecution a fact of life, it is easy to see why the early church concluded that the world existed under the wrath of God and was doomed to destruction. Anything earthy, material, or physical was, by this understanding, unfit for holy habitation.

This world view informed not only the church's preaching, but its painting as well. Christian art in the Middle Ages pictured Jesus as an effeminate man with a halo adorning his head, which obscured the fact that he could command the allegiance of other men and was physically attractive to women who, the record indicates, flocked around him during his ministry. The church has never had any trouble affirming Jesus as the Son of God with connections in heavenly places, but it has had great difficulty affirming him as a man of the earth—the Son of man—a title that completely dropped out of use in the early Christian community.

Church officials are usually disturbed if ministerial candidates do not confess Jesus as the Son of God, the second person in the Trinity, but seem to care less about ensuring the confession that he is the Son of man. If we truly believe that the divine nature was embodied in Jesus, then we must also take seriously John's assertion that carnality is, indeed, the essential attribute of the eternal God. Nor can we afford to forget that when God became flesh, our understanding of our own carnal nature was necessarily altered.

As with dancing, we must follow God's lead. We are called to be carnal. In the Christian West, however, theology has frequently been a disembodied enterprise. It has been understood as a rational discipline of the mind, and the spiritual journey has all too often become a head trip. There have, of course, been exceptions. Among some of the medieval mystics, and later in the evangelical and charismatic movements, emotions have been accorded a primary place in religious experience. But even in most of the exceptions to an excessively cognitive theology, there continues to lurk a deep suspicion of our sexual nature.

For the most part, traditional Christian theology has held that the manner in which the grace of God enters the human experience is through the preaching of God's word and the administration of the church's sacraments. Christian theology has traditionally considered matters of the flesh as less important, and certainly less godly, than things of the mind or spirit. For nineteen hundred years orthodox thinkers in the Western church have either based their understanding of God on scripture or the tradition of the church.

Generally speaking, Protestants have believed that divine truth is revealed in the Bible, a book that has come to be known as the "word of God." Some denominations believe it to be the "only infallible rule of faith and practice," "the unique and authoritative" word of God.

What has been true of the Protestant Church has also been true in the Roman Catholic tradition. Papal pronouncements, conciliar decisions, and Thomistic thought have become the building blocks for all theological discussion. They are the revealed truth, unique and authoritative for Catholic faith and practice. For mainline Western Christians, God's word is a given—either in the church's tradition or in scripture.

It follows, then, that Christian truth is not something that believers discover in human—that is, carnal—experience, much less within themselves. It is rather something that believers extract from what has already been given to the church.

The procedure for extraction is a rational process whereby ideas are linked together logically, beginning with what is given. The end result is called a "systematic theology," which proceeds from a basic premise or governing idea such as the sovereignty of God, salvation by faith, or an ascending order of reality from natural to spiritual. The Holy One is spoken of, not in the anthropomorphic terms of biblical imagery, but in the rational or conceptual categories of philosophic thought. God is all-wise and all-powerful, all-knowing and ever present. In systematic theology, God is understood as possessing superlative qualities which, while unattainable for us as mere mortals, are, nonetheless, conceivable to our minds.

That truth can be taught and apprehended by the human mind is a basic assumption underlying the model of Christian ministry that requires an educational standard for its clergy. Truth is thought to be objective. It is "out there." It is external to us. The good reverend is a scholar, a preacher, and a teacher; and he or she has the academic credentials to prove it. Sermons are expositions of scripture, and preaching seeks to instill correct beliefs in the minds of listeners. The minister knows something by virtue of his or her education that church members do not. The result is unfortunate. Faith formation tends to become a cerebral affair. Intellectual propositions are offered as truth and accepted by belief.

Historically, religious education in both the Sunday church school and weekday parochial school has been heavy on academic content and short on human experience. It has approached the teaching task as if the faith were a body of facts to be learned, Bible verses to be memorized, theological statements to be understood, names, dates, and events to be grasped. Students were catechized; that is, they were taught correct answers to stipulated questions. Today, a variety of creative means, such as audiovisuals, activities, and colorful pictures, are sometimes employed to carry out this teaching. But no matter how creative the means may be, they are used to teach knowledge about the Christian faith. The end result of such education turns out to be learning about the Bible, about the church, about God; but rarely is it a communication of Christian religious experience.

Christian educators could well take a page from the teaching manual of the Most High. When it came time for the divine disclosure, God did not offer another sermon nor a new edition of the written law. No, "the Word became flesh," says John, "and dwelt among us . . . we have beheld his glory . . ." (John 1:14). That is to say, we saw him, we touched him, we experienced him with our senses—this man of grace who was the very Word of God in our midst—we experienced him carnally. The Most High did not offer us more knowledge about divine matters. We were treated to real, honest-to-God knowledge of the Most High in Jesus. In him we see the meaning of the words "created in the image of God," an image which, by divine decree, has been inscribed and fixed within our carnal nature and is, therefore, a part of each one of us. God can only be known by embracing our own humanity.

There is a pervasive inclination among many to deny that flesh enters into the essential definition of human nature, much less that of God. Undoubtedly, the reason we have so much trouble with the humanity of Jesus is because we have such great difficulty with our own. We are embarrassed by it!

The motion picture star, Catherine Deneuve, was once interviewed after filming a picture in which she had to play some of the scenes nude. Her response is revealing.

> "I'm shy, extremely shy. I could never empty my handbag in front of anyone. I find it so excruciating to play nude scenes. For *Belle de Jour*, in the most difficult scenes, to overcome my modesty I had to take a few strong drinks. One must always help oneself to reach where one must go. I got there I hope, but it was hell.
>
> "I don't even run around naked in my own house very much. I don't think there are many actresses to whom nude, very explicit physical love scenes come easy.
>
> "There's a simple reason for female reluctance. Clothes are like a new virginity, but, above all, not that many women are proud of their nude bodies."[11]

True of women! True of men! Not many of us are that proud of our bodies—or our humanity. We are embarrassed by it.

Marilyn Monroe must have had such people in mind when she

said, in an interview shortly before her death, "We are all born sexual creatures, thank God, but it is a pity so many people despise and crush this natural gift."[12]

As a result of this embarrassment, the Christian religion has dissected human nature into something called "body and soul," and argued that the soul is where the real action is. "The soul," we say, "is immortal." Long after the body is gone, the soul will live on in eternity. God's only real interest is the soul. The body is a problem, if not *the* problem.

Moreover, we not only have dissected human nature, but also have set it against itself: the body versus the soul. We experience the split between earth and heaven as a personal dualism of soul and body. We sense two different natures, which may live together in an uneasy truce, but which are frequently in conflict. They are essentially foreign to each other, and in the case of faith, are even antagonistic to each other. Hence the tug of war between "flesh" and "spirit."

Because of this paranoia about the physical, sex has gotten bad press from the church for nineteen centuries, and monastic living has become, for some, the religious ideal. If one is serious about heaven, one must leave the world, suppress the body, and deny the self so that one is free to contemplate spiritual realities.

Inasmuch as our tendency to spiritualize the kingdom has led us to speak of the "kingdom of heaven," rather than the "kingdom of God," our understanding of divine grace has also become otherworldly. "Grace" has come to mean God's mercy that forgives us our sins so that we may enter heaven.

"Grace" is a word not often used in the Old Testament because the earthy word "shalom" covered the bases. But, like shalom, it was used as a word of greeting and blessing. "Grace to you, and peace from God our Father . . . " writes Paul in his letters to the churches. "Grace" and "shalom" carried the same meaning. Both referred to the emotional, physical, and spiritual well-being of the person or persons being addressed. Neither carried exclusively spiritual intent.

John's shocking and scandalous assertion scores a direct hit against this otherworldly spirituality. The Word became flesh. Jesus is God incarnate, that is to say, Jesus is God in carnal form. God's grace is to be understood carnally because that is how it comes to us.

Our own experience verifies John's assertion. Grace comes to us through our physical senses. It comes to us carnally. We are drawn, for example, to a work of art when our senses commune with it. We respond to its color and form and are uplifted. Spirit speaks to spirit. We hear something in a piece of music that touches us deeply. Our being is touched at its very depths in some unexplainable way. Being touches being. We find joy in holding a piece of pottery in our hands.

The form of it feels good and true. Something happens that transcends the rational process. Form communicates to form, sense to sense. The experience of grace can be found in caressing winds on the face, words of friendship, or the touching of flesh by flesh.

Ours is a sensuous God, John is saying. And Jesus is the Son of this God.

The gospel writer, Luke, offers us an interesting and revealing story about Jesus, a chip off the Old Block, we might say. Simon the Pharisee had prepared a banquet for his distinguished guest, Jesus of Nazareth, the holy man of God. The story begins in a thoroughly predictable manner. Simon—a good, upstanding religious man in the community, well educated, and no doubt a civic leader—had invited a distinguished guest to dinner. He probably came home strutting, and announced to his wife, "Guess who's coming to dinner! Jesus, the mighty prophet!"/

Probably all of us can reach back into memory and pull out a similar incident when our parents invited the minister to dinner. Mother would bring out the silver service and best table linen. We were instructed to be on our best behavior. The conversation was guarded—nothing too controversial—because, after all, the guest in our home was a spiritual leader. So the dinner that Simon the Pharisee planned was to be in every respect proper. But then there was this disturbance.

> And behold, a woman of the city, who was a sinner, when she learned that [Jesus] was at table in the pharisee's house, brought an alabaster flask of ointment, and standing behind him at his feet, weeping, she began to wet his feet with her tears, and wiped them with the hair of her head, and kissed his feet, and anointed them with the ointment. Now when the pharisee who had invited him saw it, he said to himself, "If this man were a prophet, he would have known who and what sort of woman this is who is touching him, for she is a sinner" (Luke 7:37–39).

This, too, could have been predicted. After all, public figures are the targets of demonstrations. Even the President of the United States has his hecklers. But what was unexpected, and indeed most disturbing to Simon, was Jesus' reaction. The spiritual leader did not seem to mind the interruption—nor the attention of the intruder. No doubt Simon wondered who it was who had come to dinner. If a holy man could not recognize a sinner when he saw one, something must be terribly wrong. The woman made a spectacle of herself by falling all over Jesus, kissing his feet, and caressing them with the unpinned hair of her head.

Any of us, in a similar situation, would have been offended by all the touching, embarrassed by the obvious erotic overtones. Certainly we would have felt awkward at being approached by this gushy, over-painted woman of the street. With studied composure and affected benevolence, we might have responded with a clever putdown, such as "My dear, go wash yourself." We would have expected Jesus to declare her behavior inappropriate, or at least to have disapproved of it by some sort of pained glance at Simon.

But Jesus did none of these things. He sat there accepting and—it would seem—enjoying the delicious sensations, not to mention, all of her attention.

The record is clear. If Jesus is Emmanuel—that is, God with us—then we must admit ours is a scandalous God who enjoys sensuous experience.

We might, therefore, expect the word of such a God to itself be occasionally erotic as well as sensuous. And, indeed, it is!

How fair and pleasant you are,
    O loved one, delectable maiden!
You are stately as a palm tree,
    and your breasts are like its clusters.
I say I will climb the palm tree
    and lay hold of its branches.
Oh, may your breasts be like clusters of the vine,
    and the scent of your breath like apples,
And your kisses like the best wine
    that goes down smoothly,
    gliding over lips and teeth.
                    (Song of Solomon 7:6–9)

This Hebrew love song celebrates the richly sensuous love between a woman and a man. Yet in the libraries of biblical interpretation, few passages of scripture, so patently clear in their original meaning, have caused as much difficulty as this poem. Embarrassed by the possibility that sexual love could have such a prominent place in the canon, churchly scholars rushed the allegorical method of biblical interpretation to the rescue. The dominant explanation of the poem held that this was an allegory of the prayerful communion of the spiritual person with God.

Dietrich Bonhoeffer was something of a voice crying in the wilderness when, in referring to the Song of Solomon, he insisted, "It is a good thing that the book is included in the Bible as a protest against those who believe that Christianity stands for the restraint of passion."[13]

D.H. Lawrence earned the disapproval of literary critics for writing such as that. "Scandalous!" they said. He frequently described the sensuous encounters between men and women in his novels and the experience of grace that can come to us in making love. Lady Chatterly, for example,

> . . . was filled . . . with an unspeakable pleasure. A pleasure which has no contact with speech. She felt herself filled with new blood, as if the blood of the man had swept into her veins like a strong, fresh, rousing wind, changing her whole self. All her self felt alive, and in motion, like the woods in Spring. She could not but feel that a new breath had swept into her body from the man, and that she was like a forest sloughing with a new, soft wind, sloughing and moving unspoken into bud. All her body felt like the dark interlacing of the boughs of an oak wood, softly humming in a wind, and humming inaudibly with the myriad . . . unfolding of buds. Meanwhile the birds had their heads laid on their shoulders and slept with delight in the vast interlaced intricacy of the forest of her body.[14]

Beautiful! A description of grace understood carnally. But D.H. Lawrence paid a high price for such writing; for daring to suggest that the body, flesh, sex could reflect anything spiritual or divine. His works were banned in his native England as well as in this country.

Yet in the New Testament, this shocking book of tales told in the name of God, we have an uncensored story of another woman who, like Lady Chatterly, received grace from the body of a man, the body of the man Jesus.

According to Luke (8:42–48), the woman was hemorrhaging. She was healed, not by anything Jesus said to her, but by reaching out and touching him. She touched his body, and grace abounded. Grace came to her carnally.

Grace comes to us through our bodies. Remember our experience during the Vietnam War when a certain picture was carried in newspapers and TV news reports all across the country? A North Vietnamese, his hands tied behind him, was standing on a street in Saigon with a South Vietnamese officer holding a gun to his head, just before the trigger was pulled in execution. Television, of course, carried the full horror of it and we saw the victim squeeze his eyes shut just before his head exploded into eternity, saw him collapse like a rag doll onto the pavement, saw his ruby black blood draining from him, like oil from a car, into a pool on the street. Instinctively, our bodies cried out in shock. We gasped and hid our eyes.

Then our minds stepped in and began to fashion a commentary. We rationalized what we had seen. "He was just a North Vietnamese. He was the enemy. He deserved to die because he and his kind were killing our boys. His government endangered our national security."

But our bodies recoiled by instinct. No rationalization could justify what we sensed in the initial shock. In that moment, before the mind stepped in with its commentary, our bodies conveyed to us the word of grace: All human life is sacred. War is blasphemy!

According to Jesus, God makes his sun rise on the good and on the evil, causes his rain to fall on the just and the unjust (Matt. 5:45). No rationalization there. No differentiation. Our bodies know that truth. Our instinctive body reaction has a reverence for the flesh of all people. Our carnal nature is in tune with God's sense of values even if our minds are not. It is only in the rationalization that the word of grace is lost.

And so the amazing affirmation of the gospel is that God trusts the carnal. It is part of the Creator's definition of our individuality. Since it is part of our definition as human beings, it is foolish if not blasphemous for us to try to hide from it by ignoring it, or, worse, covering it up with a spirituality that pretends to be more religious about it than God. We do just that very thing when we presume that our sexuality and our faith are mutually exclusive or, at least, unrelated.

The Most High trusts the body, trusts the sensual, trusts the sexual. The Holy One has made them vehicles of divine revelation. Carnality and revelation are not only compatible, says John, they are essential to one another. The Word became flesh—that is, carnal—and dwelt among us, full of grace and truth. God cannot do without the carnal. Nor can we. If the Most High trusts the body, the sensuous, the sexual, the earthy, so can we. We can live joyously in our bodies.

Chapter Ten

"S" Is for Sex

The most obvious differentiating characteristic about us as human beings—far more obvious than the color of our hair, the clothes we wear, or the set of our jaws—is our gender. We are male or female. And the most obvious implication of this difference is an act in which we combine our difference as male and female with our similarity as human beings—something we call "sexual intercourse."

An alien from another planet might wonder: What is the purpose of this similarity and difference in our being? What is the meaning of this union of two persons? If our alien visitor had a religious bent, he, she, or it might wonder: What did God have in mind by creating us male and female with the possibility of, and desire for, sexual intercourse?

Parents and teachers, preachers and politicians have offered answers to these questions. Their attempts are the basis of sexual morality in all cultures on this or any other planet. But we face a dilemma. Ours is a society that no longer has clear, agreed-upon answers to moral questions. Homosexuality is at least out of the closet, if not totally accepted, as an alternative sexual preference to heterosexuality. On it the wisdom of the church is divided, while on traditional sexuality the voice of the church has been muted. The puritanical attitudes of the past have been eroded.

Nevertheless, we are called by God to be carnal and to live in our bodies as sexual creatures. Space prohibits addressing the issue of homosexuality; perhaps another time, another place. But the fact remains: heterosexuality is in trouble. In our culture, sex is among the largest box office attractions and is used to sell everything on Madison Avenue from deodorants to dishwashers. Neither the repression of the past nor the exploitation of the present is of much help in answering the question of the meaning of our sexuality.

The church, when it is not warning us of its dangers, pronounces the purpose of sex to be procreation—begetting children and assuring the continuation of the species. This view of sexuality, while commendable, was forged by the church from the dualistic views of the Greco-Roman world in the second and third centuries. Learned thinkers assigned a higher order of reality to things of the mind and spirit. Things of the body, which, of course, includes our sexuality, were seen as part of an inferior order of reality and hence "sinful" in nature. Augustine equated a man's semen with sin and argued that its fertilization of the woman was the means by which original sin contaminated every generation. Even love and passion were viewed with suspicion.

The end result was a spiritual perspective on sex that, while allowing for its necessity as the means of procreation, nevertheless regarded it as dangerous and dirty. The religious ideal offered to believers by the church called for renunciation of the world and pilgrimage down the path of chastity, demanding along the way vows of poverty and obedience. If you really wanted to make it with God, you did not get married because married people do that nasty four-letter-word thing. Married couples were grudgingly given credit for continuing the human race but the church's doctrine of sex boiled down to "nasty but necessary," a view that remained unchallenged in polite society until quite recently.

Understandably, opposing voices were raised by counterculture movements of one kind or another to protest this negative view. There was the idealization of sexuality in the Middle Ages by courtly troubadours and the speak-easy allure of sinful sex during the flapper era. But not until the sixties, with their direct challenge to conventional authority, was the church's doctrine replaced in the public's mind. The new voice spoke more positively about human sexuality and affirmed it as not merely procreation, but recreation. "Sex is enjoyable and can be a lot of fun," its prophets proclaimed. Hugh Hefner articulated a philosophy of the carefree life, praising the virtue of wine, women, and song. *Playboy* and *Penthouse* became the generally acknowledged exponents of the "new" morality.

It was not long, however, until the feminist movement, its radar rotating, spotted the chauvinism at the core of the new view. The great fallacy in the phallic philosophy of the playboy is that his understanding of sexuality inevitably depersonalizes sex. The sex partner becomes an object to be used and enjoyed like fine wine, good food, and a sporty car. In a consumer society, people, like things, become disposable items to be used, enjoyed, and discarded. The playmate of the month is a toy to be played with and measured—36-24-36—but not a person to whom the playboy would relate, much less to whom he would commit himself. Her personality, talents, and views on social issues are of no concern. His interest in her goes no further than her body which, like other commodities in a consumer society, is enjoyed temporarily.

Because sex has to do with recreation rather than procreation, it enjoys none of the safeguards surrounding family responsibilities such as a public declaration of commitment. The relationship that develops between playmates will endure only as long as each desires it and this, in turn, usually depends upon remaining young and sexually attractive.

115

If a "serious relationship" is entered into, it rests on the shifting sands of emotional attachment and has none of the social approval provided by a wedding ceremony. Consequently, in addition to becoming impersonal, recreational sex tends to be irresponsible. The persons involved feel they must remain free with no strings attached.

One fact is abundantly clear: The established authorities have been deposed. We have wandered from the garden, and the gate has slammed shut behind us. In a dilemma similar to that of Hansel and Gretel, away from home and lost in the forest, we are uncertain about which way to turn. We are not sure where we are going, but we are certainly on our way.

But just before darkness overtakes us, an unrecognized, yet strangely familiar voice is heard coming over our shoulder. Like a long-forgotten relative from childhood recollection, the storyteller of scripture turns up with a yarn to spin.

Elaine Pagels contends that from the second century on, the Genesis story of creation became for Christians as well as Jews,

> . . . a primary means for revealing and defending basic attitudes and values. Our spiritual ancestors argued and speculated over how God had commanded the first man and woman to "be fruitful and multiply, and fill the earth," and how he instituted the first marriage; how Adam, after he found among the animals no "helper fit for him" . . . met Eve, with well-known and disastrous consequences. Such interpretations . . . engaged intensely practicle [sic] concerns and articulated deeply felt attitudes.[15]

The story beckons. Perhaps a return to that "primary" source of "basic attitudes and values" can shed some light on our situation. The tale recognizes the procreational fruit of sexual union and the earthy enjoyment of its attraction and consummation, but it locates the purpose of our sexuality beyond both. Not procreation. Not recreation. But revelation. Human sexuality is intended to demonstrate and declare the meaning of relationship. It is a means by which I come to understand the meaning of my "I-ness," your "Thou-ness," and our "We-ness."

The familiar Genesis story, retold here with a few literary liberties taken, is, I think, both interesting and revealing. The narrative portrays the Creator of the universe as one who, after many days of sweaty labor, wanted to celebrate the awesome accomplishment. So God called out to a freshly created oak tree, "Let's the two of us go out and have a drink to celebrate the wonder of little acorns and big oak trees." Well, the oak tree just stood there stiff and silent with its leaves fluttering in the breeze. It made no reply to God's invitation.

116

Somewhat perplexed, the Holy One sidled up to a horse, still wet from the Creator's hand, and said, "Good morning! How's about you and me celebrating the beauty of this day and the warmth of the sun on your strong back?" And figuring that something was lacking in the first divine invitation, God added, "And I'm buying! The drinks are on me." But the horse just stood there, looking confused. It pawed the earth with shiny hooves and swished its long silky tail to chase the newly created flies away. But the horse said nothing.

Now anyone who can create a world in six days has to have a lot of determination, and God was not one to give up easily. Besides, the Creator's thirst was growing. So God nudged a mountain into existence and said to it, "Look at that! I just squeezed you up from a mere mole hill. Doesn't that astound you?" But the mountain just stood there looking majestic with its granite head in the clouds—silent as stone.

God was truly puzzled. In fact, God had never before been so frustrated. Of course, God had never before created a universe, and there were bound to be some bugs in the grand design. Nevertheless, the Almighty was perplexed. More important, God was lonely. "I may have goofed!" God said. "In this whole creation there isn't anything that can relate to me. Not one thing with whom I can talk or break bread."

So God said, "I must create something in my very own image—something that is capable of relating to me, something that can laugh with me, argue with me, celebrate with me." And it was then that God blew some dust from under the bed and, thereby, created one more creature. God created humankind, and called it "Adam."

Now the story repeats itself.

Adam awoke and stretched. He marveled at all the wonders of creation as they passed before his eyes and was, himself, delighted with his good fortune to be part of the grand parade. "It's great to be alive," he said to no one in particular. "I think I'll celebrate." Adam approached the oak tree, the horse, and the mountain with a similar invitation and no more success at securing a companion for his party than God had achieved before him. "I'm lonely," Adam declared.

God, who was standing nearby and had observed all of Adam's frustrated efforts, overheard him. "Yes, I know the feeling," God sympathized. "But I've had some experience in these matters. Don't worry! Be happy!" which is to say, "Lie down, take a nap, and when you wake up I'll have a big surprise for you. Trust me!"

And Adam did trust God, and he did take a nap. When he awoke he discovered, much to his delight, that God had created yet one more creature. But it was not another man. True, this creature was more like Adam than different; yet, she was different. She was woman. She was Eve.

The first thing Adam and Eve did was to go, arm and arm, out on the town. A celebration was in order. They enjoyed one another's company.

The second thing they did was to invite God over to their place for Sunday dinner. Just as the man and woman were more alike than different, yet distinctive, so God and humankind remain more alike than different, yet distinctive. They, too, can enjoy one another's company.

The story suggests that in this similarity and difference lies the possibility of relationship. The capacity for human relationship with God lies in the similarity we share with the Holy One, just as the potential for relationship between a man and a woman exists in the similarity of their being. Our relationship with God is not merely that of creature to Creator, something that all the products of God's creative energy share in common; it is that of person to Person.

The frank anthropomorphic depictions of God in the Old Testament—walking in the garden, smelling incense, displaying feelings of anger and jealousy—these are not the result of a primitive mind, as if modern God-talk were more advanced because it uses conceptual, sexless language. These early depictions represent, rather, an essential part of the Hebrew understanding of the nature of God. We have more in common with God than do rocks and trees and animals.

Yet the meaning of our relationship lies in the difference between us and God. We are human beings, not gods. It is God who has made us and not we ourselves. The distinction is both crucial and informative because the clue to human identity is rooted in our sexuality.

Let us pause long enough to note a literary characteristic of Old Testament poetry. An idea or thought is stated in one line of verse, then repeated in the next using different words. Thus:

> The earth is the LORD's, and the fulness thereof,
> > the world and those who dwell therein;
> for he has founded it upon the seas,
> > and established it upon the rivers.
> > > (Ps. 24:1, 2)

This characteristic of parallel construction in Hebrew poetry equates human sexuality with the image of God. The Genesis storyteller is saying that to be created in the image and likeness of God is to be created male and female.

> God created man in his own image,
> > in the image of God he created him;
> male and female he created them.
> > (Gen. 1:27)

When God created man, he made him in the likeness of God.
Male and female he created them,
and he blessed them and named them Man when they were created.
(Gen. 5:1, 2)

The storyteller believes that, through their gender, Adam and Eve are to understand themselves as God's creatures. Just as they are similar, yet different, so God, who is also like them, is yet distinctively different. By sharing their similarity as human beings and uniting their uniqueness as male and female, they experience themselves as relational creatures reflecting the image of God. It is in their sexual life that they know their essential nature. They have been created as close companions for each other and for God.

The Genesis story is significant for a worldly spirituality because it suggests that our identity has been defined for us by our Creator and rooted in our sexuality. We are sexual beings, created as such in the image of God. Our lives can only find meaning as sexual beings. God defines the nature of human existence and we must not be more spiritual about it than our Creator. We cannot pretend that our sexuality does not matter nor that it is something we must transcend or deny. Our understanding of ourselves and our Creator are inextricably bound to our sexuality. The nature of our humanity lies in the givenness of our sexuality, which reflects the image of God. The clues to the meaning of life are not found in the chapel or the classroom but in the bedroom. We have been designed for personal relationship with each other and with our Maker.

The story assumes that this personal relationship is part of the created order of things. The Genesis narrator speaks of it by using the image of Eve being taken from the side of Adam, formed from one of his ribs. When he discovers Eve by his side, he acknowledges this unity by exclaiming, "This at last is bone of my bones and flesh of my flesh" (Gen. 2:23). The story makes it clear that "Adam"—which, in the Hebrew, let us remember, means "human race"—is such only as he is male and female, only as he has Eve as his companion. He is not fully God's definition of humanity unless, and until, Adam is constituted male and female. The one complements and supplements the other.

A spirituality of sexuality has profound psychological implications for our mental health. Only as we acknowledge and accept both the masculine and the feminine within ourselves can there be wholeness of personality.

Sociologically, a spirituality of sexuality has implications for feminist concerns. We must say that man and woman together make up the wholeness of God's definition of humankind. There is an essential unity, and hence, equality between them inherent in their creaturely natures. In their sexual differences and the union of these differences through intercourse, they realize their created unity or one-ness. This one-ness is of divine design. It is the one-ness of relationship and constitutes the functional meaning of the "image of God."

The sexual relationship of Adam and Eve, reveals in the clearest way the nature of relationship. As they stand before God with all of their human similarities and differences, they experience the same kind of one-ness with God that they do in their sexual relationship. Their sexual life is given to them as a divine demonstration and declaration of the meaning of relationship. In its created intention, Adam brings his "I-ness" to the sexual union, even as Eve brings her "Thou-ness." Neither loses the integrity of being in the act; neither the "I-ness" of Adam nor the "Thou-ness" of Eve is lost. Yet both are transcended in something we might call their "We-ness." A new bonding comes into being, which the Bible speaks of as "one flesh."

Similarly, in the relationship with God, neither our "I-ness" nor God's "Thou-ness" is denied, but a unique bond of intimacy is established between human creatures and Creator. The Bible speaks of it as "abiding" in God (cf. John 15:4). "You and me, Lord!" "We-ness."

But, alas, there is more to the story. They did not live happily ever after. With all the loving and hugging going on in the garden of Eden between the folks and God, the question was bound to come up sooner or later. Who raised it, the storyteller does not say, nor does it matter. Let us suppose Adam did. Adam must have said something like, "I understand the similarity between us, God, but what is the difference?"

"Good question!" said the Holy One. Actually the question caught God by surprise, since it had never been raised before. So God took a minute to think, which in Adam's time must have seemed like an eternity. Finally God replied, "You and I are so much alike that we can eat the fruit from any of the trees in this garden. But just to keep things simple, let's agree that you can eat the fruit from all the trees except that one over yonder."

Seemed like a good idea at the time. "I get the idea," Adam said. "That tree is off limits to us so we will remember there is a difference between you as Creator, and Eve and me as human beings."

Well, you remember the rest of the story. Adam was not very enterprising and, left to himself, would probably have turned out to be a pretty dull fellow. Eve, on the other hand, had an eye for fashion and color, a taste for adventure, and a whole lot of gumption. She and Adam climbed the fence around that tree, ate some of its fruit and started hallucinating. They noticed for the first time they were naked as two jaybirds. But worse, they were embarrassed by it and tried to cover themselves by hiding from each other and from God. It was a feeling they had never experienced before. They felt awkward and self-conscious, and it put considerable strain on their lovemaking, not to mention, their relationship with the Almighty. Of course, they did not realize it yet, but they had just invented "Sin."

Biblically understood, sin is broken relationship. The story suggests that the Creator's part in the divine drama is to set the terms of existence for the creation. God defines the meaning of our existence as relational creatures. Within the divine definition our lives have meaning. Outside of it we do not know who we are. Consequently, we are driven to play the role of the Creator ourselves by devising a definition of our own humanity. The results prove disastrous; or so the story goes.

Adam and Eve, by ignoring the divine definition of their humanity stepped into God's shoes, thereby creating their own identity. They were, in fact, playing God. But the shoes were too big. Wearing them created blisters. They destroyed the very essence of the "I-Thou" relationship intended by God, and instead, produced one characterized by "I-It" for all the parties involved.

It is to the narrator's credit that sin is defined functionally rather than moralistically. Adam and Eve hide from God in the bushes. Adam blames Eve for all the trouble, and Eve passes the buck to the snake. Eve loathes snakes and mice and other creepy, crawly creatures, and must now bear children in pain, while Adam, who is frustrated in his farming efforts by a crop of thistles, exercises dominion over his helpmate. All of these actions are portrayed as the result of sin and not the Creator's intention.

We must note in passing that the Genesis bard has portrayed Adam's dominion over Eve as the result of sin. In an age when these mythic stories were told from a patriarchal perspective, such a liberated point of view, embedded in the text, is quite remarkable.

In any case, sin, functionally understood, is broken relationship. Its symptoms are shame, embarrassment, envy, jealousy, anger, selfishness, competition, murder—all the dynamics that disrupt and destroy human relationships. But it disrupts not only the relationships we have with other human beings, it fractures the relationship between Creator and creature, humanity and nature, and even causes an alienation within ourselves. All of these relationships suffer from the sin of estrangement.

In telling the story, the author has held up a mirror for us that reflects the reality of our situation. Sin has alienated us not only from God and each other, but from our environment as well. The ozone layer is being depleted, thereby increasing exposure to the sun and the risk of skin cancer. Dead seals are being washed up along the shores of Alaska, the victims of oil spills. Animal and plant species are becoming extinct because of human greed.

We trivialize sin when we think of it in moralistic categories. "I don't smoke, and I don't chew. And I don't go with girls who do!" Sin has to do with broken relationship. Murder and war, theft and rape are only the more obvious and extreme forms of it.

A few nights ago I was having dinner with my family. Spaghetti was on the menu, and it was delicious. Understandably, my wife wanted a second helping and asked me to pass the bowl. I reached for it and noticed that the spaghetti had drooped over the edge, leaving the rim greasy except for a spot just big enough for my thumb. I turned the bowl until I could pick it up at that point, and handed it to my wife. She had to take hold of the greasy rim. My hand was spared.

Trivial, you say! But that is just how subtle sin is. Before God's indictment, Adam offered up his helpmate as the scapegoat. "The woman whom thou gavest to be with me, she gave me fruit of the tree, and I ate" (Gen. 3:12). Sound familiar? In the universe of our dining room, I was willing to sacrifice my wife's hands so that I might remain undefiled. Both Adam and I were creating a universe in our own image. No longer content to be merely human, we were hell-bent on playing God and making the universe fit our specifications. For that moment, at least, the relationship between my wife and me must be characterized as "I-It" rather than "I-Thou."

I think of my childhood and the summers at camp. Mealtimes would find us with ravenous appetites. Seated on benches at the dinner table, each camper would pull impatiently at the bench trying to get close to the table where the food waited to satisfy our hunger. But, of course, with each of us pulling at a different time, the bench did not move. Not until we pulled together could our meal begin. As long as each of us organized the universe around ourselves, the results violated the law of supply and demand.

Such is the subtlety of sin and the broken relationships that result. As pretenders to the throne of grace, we create disunity out of unity, alienation in the place of cooperation. Separation has replaced the oneness of Eden.

Tragically, our created humanity has been destroyed at the heart of what was once the essence of it: our sexuality. Our eyes have been opened. But instead of being drawn together in love, we see the other as the object of lust to be used, or we feel threatened by open, honest nakedness and, hence, hide behind masks to cover it.

The value of our cultural fixation on sex is to remind us that we are, in fact, sexual creatures, created as such by no less than God. But one of the glaring deficiencies in the popular understanding of sexuality is that it does not take sin, that is broken relationship, seriously. It would have us believe that "love, just love," is the only requirement for making the world go round, and that people can jump in and out of bed with ease, there to discover, ah, the sweet mystery of life.

But sin is a fact of life, and it cannot be ignored or wished away. Shame is the telltale sign that neither fantasy nor fiction can erase. Shame is the indelible recollection of our estrangement from the garden of Eden. Shame is the flaming sword that stands at Eden's gate, barring our entry. It is the reminder that we live in disunity with God, the world, ourselves, and each other.

A rather depressing picture!

But fortunately there is still more to the story.

We have noted earlier that basic to the Christian faith is the portrayal of God as a Creator who is at work fashioning a new heaven and earth, otherwise known as "the kingdom of God." Seen in light of our sexual story, we could speak of this activity as a restoration of the "garden of Eden."

As believers, we must not forget that it was the Creator God who was in Christ reconciling the world to himself (cf. 2 Cor. 5:19). The operative word in Paul's claim is "reconciling." It is a relational term. Functionally, it means, God was in Christ restoring the relationships of creature and Creator, humanity and environment, friend and enemy, man and woman. God was in Christ opening again the gates of Eden.

Because we live by the stories we tell ourselves, it is important that we, as believers, give some thought to how we tell the creation story and particularly, the re-creation story, the Jesus story. An architect once told me, "If you build a house, you will want to spend plenty of time designing it. Be sure it's the kind of home you want to live in, because once it's built, the home will design you." So with faith stories. What we come to believe as truth molds our lives.

When Paul speaks of Jesus as the "Second Adam" (1 Cor. 15:47), he offers us a powerful image for telling the re-creation story and shaping our understanding of human sexuality.

In Christ the believer sees the re-creation of God's original definition of "Adam." But Jesus needs no one taken from his side to complete his wholeness as Person. In Christ we see the oneness of Adam and Eve. In his personhood the unity of God's original creative intention is revealed. In him, God's Word, or definition of relationship, is declared restored. God and creature, humanity with the world, people with themselves and each other, and, of course, woman and man. "In Christ," says Paul, "there is neither Jew nor Greek, neither slave nor free, neither male nor female, for we have all become one [flesh] in him" (cf. Gal. 3:28). From this perspective, the Jesus story is God's promise to us and gives us permission to believe that restored relationship, in all of its comfortable nakedness, is once again a possibility.

The gospel story proclaims the kingdom of God's shalom as having come in Christ. The kingdom of God is the garden of Eden, and Jesus, as the Second Adam, stands at the gates bidding us come follow him into its midst. Eden has been reopened. The Temple veil has been torn away. No longer is the entrance barred or the Holy of Holies separated from the courtyard of the Gentiles.

The myth of Eden has become historical reality in Jesus, and the story of re-creation has opened to us the genuine possibility of restored relationship. In Christ's oneness with himself, others, and God rests the assurance of our restoration to the one-flesh relationship of the Creator's intention. Christ is God's Word on it, made flesh. He is God's decision regarding us, our humanity, and our sexuality. The alienation of sin is broken. God triumphs. Re-created human sexuality once again nourishes the springs of our humanity. It declares the victory of Christ over sin, that is, over a world of broken relationships.

It is in our sexual coming together that we can most clearly understand what the Redeemer has done in restoring us to union with God and with one another. In our coming together as man and woman, we experience restored relationship. We understand what the oneness of an open, honest, naked relationship actually is.

Because sex demonstrates and declares Christ's triumph over sin, it is blasphemous to set sexuality and spirituality against each other, as if one were of the devil and the other of God. The Bible belongs in the bedroom. In both we discover the meaning of God's saving act in Christ.

A biblical understanding of human sexuality has much to contribute to the current cultural concern with sex. First, it sets forth a positive moral position based on the believer's understanding of the purpose of human sexuality—neither procreation nor recreation, but the re-creation of human relationships. It does not simply say, "Don't do this because you may contract a venereal disease" (a real possibility), or "Don't do that because you may become pregnant" (also a very real possibility). Christian morality rejoices in human sexuality and affirms its value. The discussion of premarital intercourse is, thereby, delivered from the moralistic categories of "right" and "wrong." Instead, morality deals with what is appropriate behavior in a developing relationship.

Obviously, playmate sex is inappropriate since its concern is with bodies, their use and enjoyment, rather than whole persons, their mystery and well-being. But equally obvious is that when two people grow in their love for one another, more and more intimate expressions of their love will become appropriate as their relationship deepens. As they develop ever-deeper levels of commitment to each other, moving from friendship and dating to going steady, engagement, and marriage, so, too, appropriate expressions of that relationship will move along a continuum from hand-holding and kissing to petting and intercourse.

Second, for the Christian couple, the primary function of sex is not procreation. Rather it is the re-creation of relationship. The "multiply and fill the earth" of Genesis 1:28 needs to be heard, not so much as a divine command to Adam and Eve—as is commonly assumed—but as a shalom blessing given by God to their sexual union with the promise of children. Procreation is the "frosting on the cake" of sex. Sexual intercourse happens to beget offspring by the grace of God, but it is not the purpose or meaning of the couple's coming together. The desire to reproduce appears in the couple as the divinely inspired wish to create a child of their own, that is, to establish a relationship with a creature created in their own image. As such, the primary function of human sexuality remains the re-creation of relationships. The awareness that human procreation is secondary to the couple's exercise of their sexuality obviously has significant positive implications for the practice of contraception and family planning.

In our society, sex has been either worshiped or whipped. But from the vantage point of the biblical storytellers, we have seen that neither is appropriate. Rather, it is to be understood and enjoyed for what God has made it.

"and God created humanity in the divine image. In the image of God they were created, male and female God created them. . . . and the Word became flesh and dwelt among us. . . ."

Chapter Eleven

"You're Not the Person I Married"

Bible stories are not fairy tales. They are the footprints of pilgrims, left on the beaches where the sacred and the secular meet. They represent the rapture of human existence and provide a map for us as we make our own spiritual journeys.

But how do these Bible stories translate into reality? And, specifically, how does the open, honest, nakedness of Eden and the re-created relationship embodied in Christ become a real possibility for us?

We must remember that the coming of Christ was itself the culmination of a long courtship of the human race by the divine Suitor. The bridge that spanned the chasm of broken relationship throughout the centuries of Old Testament history was God's covenant with Israel. Because of it the Holy One made, and kept, a commitment to reclaim her from her life as an adulterous wife. Sin in all of its destructive, alienating power could not dissuade the divine will from its monogamous faithfulness to Israel. The significance of Christ is that he comes in the context of this covenant history and enters upon the stage of history as the fulfillment of its promise, "in the fullness of time." The Second Adam, the one in whom relationships are restored to their created intention, does not appear in a vacuum. He comes as the fulfillment of the promise contained in covenant commitment.

The story suggests that open, honest, naked relationship is restored within a history of personal commitment. To a romantic culture that believes love produces beautiful relationships and justifies going to bed, the biblical narrative argues otherwise. Not love, but covenant commitment makes for great sex and restored relationship.

People seem to fall in and out of love with unnerving ease and frequency. It apparently happens so often, one stand-up comic insisted, that some Hollywood stars own drip-dry wedding gowns. More seriously, Eric Fromm reminds us that to love truly is to be able to love others, an observation that is born out in the experience of many couples. Indeed, husbands and wives fall in and out of love with each other as well as with friends and acquaintances. Despite all the hype, love proves to be an unstable glue for holding relationships together permanently or even long enough for the fullness of time to fulfill its promise.

It is *commitment*, not love, that secures a marriage relationship. This wisdom is embodied in the vows of the wedding ceremony. A man and a woman make a covenant vow in the presence of witnesses to commit themselves to each other as husband and wife in sickness and in health, in joy and in sorrow, in plenty and in want, until death does them part. Commitment is the soil in which reconciliation can grow and love will flourish.

There is a delightful line in Edith Sommer's play *Room Full of Roses*[16], in which a little girl asks her mother, "Mommy, have you ever considered divorcing Daddy?" The mother is shocked and insists, "No, never!" Then she thinks for a moment and responds with a gleam in her eyes, "Murder, yes, but never divorce."

A similar response was delivered by the Old Testament prophet, Amos, to a wayward Israel. She had been unfaithful to her covenant Partner and was about to conclude that the marriage was over. Speaking on behalf of God, Amos thundered, "You only have I known, Israel. You only have I pledged myself to. Therefore, I will sell you into bondage. Murder, yes! But never divorce" (cf. Amos 3:2).

Interestingly, the Old Testament frequently uses the marriage analogy to express the relationship between Israel and God, and when Jesus speaks of an "adulterous generation" (Matt. 12:39), he is not referring to sexual misdemeanors but to transgressions of the divine marriage between the Holy One and the people.

It is, then, within the "locked-in-ness" of God's covenant relationship to Israel that the Christ finally comes. Christ is the reconciling one, the one who restores broken relationship, the Second Adam who opens again the gates of the garden where vulnerable nakedness before God and each other becomes comfortable. Within the context of a covenant commitment, the reconciliation of this man and this woman into the one flesh of Christ takes place.

The restoration of which the Jesus story speaks does not come overnight. It is not the result of "one-night stands." Rather, it comes in the "fullness of time," in the give-and-take of a covenant history. Marriage serves as the covenant that provides the history in which the one flesh of Christ can be realized by a woman and a man.

It is, of course, possible for a covenant of commitment to exist between a couple apart from marriage. There, too, Christ can come in the "fullness of time." Nevertheless, marriage partners enjoy a social reinforcement of their commitment that couples merely living together do not. Conversely, some marriages not only fail to bring forth the

Christ in their history, but actually deepen the gulf of estrangement between the partners. Still, for most Christians, God's covenant with Israel—and all the struggle that it meant for both of them—offers the best model for understanding marriage.

Believers come to the covenant of marriage with a unique understanding of what it means to be a sexual creature. Marital sex bears witness to the redemptive act of God, accomplished in Christ as the Second Adam. A worldly spirituality will urge Christian couples to practice becoming great lovers. If it is true that our sexual life reveals the meaning of what God has done in Christ, then we must remove any obstacle that prevents or obscures that understanding. Derrick Sherwin Bailey believes,

> Every sexual act is at once an accurate reflection of, and a judgment upon, a couple's whole relation. Any incompatibility between the ideal and the actual is experienced as a tension which disturbs their intercourse and indicates that they are failing to work out satisfactorily in the life of everyday all that 'one flesh' implies. They must therefore pay careful heed to the quality of their relation as it is made known to them in their coming together, for the sexual act will always be either a joyful affirmation of their common life, or a revelation of its defects.[17]

Christian marriage, and its sexual expression, can become, thereby, a model of the kingdom of God. Developing our ability to make great love becomes a joyful spiritual discipline for the couple because their sex life can never be regarded as insignificant in light of that kingdom which it can demonstrate and declare.

There is a sacramental quality about marital sex. For the believer, sexual intercourse is both the sign and the seal of re-created relationship. It is a foretaste of kingdom living, where, having attained the likeness of Jesus, we will, as he said, have no need to be given to one another in marriage (Luke 20:35). Our sexual union anchors the gospel message in our experience. Through monogamous intercourse, we receive the sign of what the one-flesh state of being is. In our vulnerable, yet comfortable, nakedness, we learn to reveal both our inner as well as our outer selves to our mates without mask or pretense.

But marital sex is not only the sign or foretaste of this restored unity, but also a guarantee or seal of it. To experience the oneness of Christ with my spouse is to know—at least theoretically—that it is possible to experience oneness with everyone. The worldly fact of paradise regained is experienced as partners come together in sexual openness and nakedness. Intercourse within the context of covenant commitment can demonstrate and declare the meaning of all human relationships. Husbands and wives are people who are learning how to be open and trusting with each other—and with others. Spouses practice loving—giving and receiving emotional shalom. This is the learned lesson of marriage that is to be shared with every human being. Marital sex exists to remind us continually that we have been created in the image of God, that is, for relationship with all of God's creatures. Eric Fromm observes,

> Love . . . is never restricted to one person. If I can love only one person and nobody else, if my love for one person makes me more alienated and distant from my fellow man, I may be attached to this person in any number of ways, but I do not love.[18]

Christian marriage is the minor league in which we are trained to play in the major leagues of God's kingdom. I learn from my wife what it means to live as a human being in relationship with others. With her, I learn how to venture vulnerability before others. In her presence, I experience the openness that I am called upon to risk in the world. I practice the sharing with her from which others will benefit. Because we experience this oneness in our relationship together, we know that one day, in the fullness of time, we too will be able to relate to all of God's people without mask or pretense in the comfortable nakedness of our humanity, even as Jesus did. Our faith in Christ is anchored in our experience as a couple.

The question inevitably arises: Does not the Jesus story, with its promise of reconciliation, break up on the shoals of current divorce statistics? The figures do not paint a very bright picture for the institution of marriage, Christian or otherwise. They are all the more disturbing when we realize that no one is married intending to get a divorce. Most marriages begin in an atmosphere of genuine affection and commitment. The flowers are fresh and the hopes are high for the future. In my experience as a pastor, I have yet to marry a couple who were not rapturously in love and absolutely certain that the future was secure in that love. The verbalizations of love may be somewhat naive and lack experience, but typically I hear such expressions as: "My fiance has the same tastes that I do." "We never fight." "We are so much alike, we agree on everything." "Even before we say something we know what the other is thinking."

The numbers would not be so disturbing if people entered marriage with their fingers crossed behind their backs. Perhaps then we could understand why the number of divorces is increasing at such an alarming rate. What ought to give us pause is that one out of two of these rapturously in love couples, who are so sure of the future, and who apparently agree on everything, is headed for a separation or divorce.

Why? What happens?

Marriage counselors tell us that marriages go through stages of development just as people do. After the honeymoon phase of marriage is over—which can last up to six years—a period of disillusionment follows, giving rise to the cliché, "Love is blind, but marriage is an eye-opener." Couples come to the disturbing realization that they are not nearly as similar as they once thought. They discover differences that at first were intriguing and enjoyable but, as the years pile up, become increasingly disturbing and irritable. The naive belief that all differences can be resolved by talking things over is fantasy. Although communication is the basic skill to develop in a marital relationship, sometimes its practice only serves to reveal how deep the differences run. As the masks are taken off and the gloves are put on, those differences are seen more clearly and demand attention. Finally, the painful truth is acknowledged, "You are not the person I married."

It is at this point in the relationship that the marriage faces its most severe crisis.

Statistically, we know that half of the couples conclude, "Since you are not the person I married there is no point in continuing the marriage," and end up in a divorce court.

An untold number of the remaining couples choose to ignore the differences that separate them. After an uneasy truce in which life is compartmentalized, the communication across the boundaries comes to an end. The two continue living together but have purchased serenity at the price of emotional separation.

There is, however, a third alternative, one that takes massive courage and determination to choose. It involves great risk as it climbs uphill through tangles of pain and the labyrinths of change. It is the alternative of living with the reality of differences and daring to see them as gifts brought to the relationship. When the halo is gone and disillusionment has set in, the work of building a great marriage can begin. Great marriages are not made in heaven, as we might like to believe, but by two people who—by God!—determine to make a great marriage.

Christian spirituality can offer help for the climb. It offers insights about the nature of human relationships, which both ground us in reality and make available for our use the symbols of the Jesus story.

Part of the romantic myth of our culture, believed at least by lovers, is that people are compatible and, therefore, get married. It is commonly assumed that compatibility is a basic requirement for marriage and maintaining the relationship. Therefore, when the couple discovers their incompatibility, the scenario has it that they get a divorce. When disillusionment has set in and they are beginning to see each other as they really are, the world draws the conclusion, "Consequently . . . ," and offers divorce as the remedy.

The Christian faith, on the other hand, begins with the assumption that we are fundamentally incompatible. Incompatibility is normal. Compatibility is a gift of grace and hard work. Putting it another way, compatibility is the result of marriage rather than a reason for it. The Bible, as we have seen, calls this basic incompatibility "sin" and assumes it to be an essential part of the human definition. But whether we call it "incompatibility," "sin," "self-centeredness," or simply "idiosyncrasy," in all marriages we need to take into account the elements of incompatibility that are always lurking in the shadows.

Oddly enough, it is our very incompatibilities that make us interesting people. Sameness, like perfection, would be boring. Nevertheless, we spend a good deal of time trying to create perfection in others, if not in ourselves. I have been married to one woman for thirty-five years. This morning when I finished shaving, I reached for the towel to dry my face. The towel was gone. It had been thrown into the laundry last night by my good wife. For thirty-five years she has been gathering the towels and washing them and for thirty-five years she has never put a towel back on the rack. For thirty-five years she has known that I like to dry my face when I am finished shaving. For thirty-five years I have tried to reform her to my specifications and for thirty-five years she has stubbornly refused to change one iota in this regard.

Of course, for thirty-five years my wife has had to put up with the residual effects of a conditioned male chauvinism. The lesson which thirty-five years of marital schooling has taught us is that if we cannot love each other with our faults, we cannot love each other with our virtues. The two are inseparably entwined. If I cannot learn to let my wife be herself with all of her idiosyncrasies and differences and without crushing her into my mold—creating her in my image—then there is no truth to the faith I profess. I have no reason to assume that the next thirty-five years will be any different than the first; at least with regard to my wife's remembering to put a towel on the towel bar. Nor does she expect me to change my chauvinistic peeve. If we cannot love the tares in each other's life, we cannot love the wheat either.

I am indebted to my father for many things, but one of the gifts I cherish most is something he said to me hours after my mother's death. He said, "Bob, you know I saw her last night bathing in the bathtub, and she was beautiful." My father thought that my seventy-six-year-old mother had a beautiful body.

Many of us seem to be obsessed with dieting and exercising in order to make ourselves acceptable to our marriage partners. We think being a good marriage partner means we must slim down, build our bodies up, and get our act together. The truth is that if we cannot love our spouses in their flabbiness, and with rolls of fat, we cannot love them in their trim firmness. We do not love a mate now and then, here or there. We love them in their ambiguous wholeness or we do not love them at all.

The differences are there! Compatibility does not come ready-made. Consequently, believers are not surprised when they discover they are not as compatible as they thought. The inevitable onslaught of disillusionment is not a counsel of cynicism or pessimism. On the contrary, the discovery that "you are not the person I married," is grounds for hope because it means that the couple can begin to live in reality. It can be an awakening because over the lament of our incompatibility the Creator God speaks the "Nevertheless . . ." of grace. The gospel word is "re-creation." Our assurance is that the Word has already become flesh once, and can do so again, as it comes to dwell among us in our homes. The enfleshed Word offers us, as believers, a promise, that in spite of all evidence to the contrary, there is a reconciling power to be found in the midst of our differences.

To those who say that love is blind but marriage is an eye-opener, we reply, "Not so! Love sees with amazing clarity; especially if it looks at life through God's eyes." Jesus' vision was a divine 20/20.

No doubt about it, the apostle Peter had a spitfire temper and the impetuosity of a schoolboy. A marriage counselor or psychiatrist would have said, "That's going to be a problem for a married man and a church leader. Better get some counseling or give up marriage and the ministry." But Jesus looked at his neurosis and saw it as a gift. He looked at the reckless Simon, but saw boldness. So he named him "Peter," which means "rock." "And on this rock," Jesus said, "I will build my church" (Matt. 16:18).

Jesus invites us to view our marriage partners this way.

The Christ of the gospels does not change us, he renames us. That is a critical distinction. He does not do away with our neuroses. He simply invites us to rename them and calls them "gifts."

God's grace does not do away with our incompatibilities anymore than it does away with the cross of Christ. The resurrection does not change the historical fact of the crucifixion, but it does give us permission to rename the cross as a symbol of life, not death. It gives us permission to call it a symbol of glory, not scandal, a symbol of atonement, not tragedy, a new beginning, not failure. It is a remarkable feat of faith that we dare to call the Friday of crucifixion, "Good Friday." The cross is not eradicated but, when we rename it, all of life's "problems" can be seen differently. The resurrection allows us to see our situation gracefully.

132

The power of the gospel is its claim of resurrection or re-creation, a claim that gives us permission to rename our foibles and flaws. Incompatibilities can be seen as gifts. Our idiosyncrasies make us interesting persons. Stubbornness can be seen as independence. Feistiness can be seen as delightful. We are not locked into the stereotypes assigned to us, nor are the labels pasted across our bumps and warts fixed.

Christian hope is not something we derive from evidence. Christian hope is something we claim contrary to the evidence and only because the Most High gives us permission, through a story, to draw contrary conclusions, i.e., to rename the data. We have God's Word on it. That Word is "Jesus Christ," born in a barn, crucified on a cross, and raised to glory. His story gives us permission to look at our lives and our marriages gracefully. Improved through the spectacles of faith, our vision enables us to see beyond what is, to what can be.

But beware! Entering marriage is a dangerous opportunity because it does not leave us as it found us. It changes us. In it and through it, we are invited by God to become new creatures. Behind the cry, "You are not the person I married," lies the exasperating awareness that the times, "they are a changin'." The only certainty that life offers us is the certainty of change itself. "You are not the person I married," is the thinly veiled wish to nail things down as they once were. It is the nostalgic reach to hold on to the past; to sit contentedly in front of life's fireplace. We had assumed we would settle down and hang out our marital shingle, "Business as usual," and, as the story goes, "live happily ever after."

So the question is: "Why? Why did you change? Why can't it always be as it was?" Not only is an accusation hidden in the question, but the accusation assumes that something terrible has happened because of the change. The change is undesirable and unfortunate so far as the marriage is concerned.

The story of Pentecost warns us that when the Spirit enters our house, it may come as a whirlwind or set us ablaze with fingers of fire. If so, some things are apt to be incinerated.

The passing of the old and the coming of the new, like the wind and the fire, is of God. And therein lies our hope. We do not need to fear the changes in our marriage partner that the erosion of years reveals. It is God that destroys the old wineskins because new ones are required to hold the fermentation of the Spirit. As married couples, wrestling with the incompatibilities of our relationship, we have divine permission to see this change as good because it can be called "growth."

Sometimes newlyweds boast, "We like the same things, and never disagree on anything," as if the condition were something about which

133

to be proud. Their claim is probably not nearly as true as young lovers would like us to believe. But if it is, God help them! That marriage will be bore-ing; dullsville, uninteresting, stagnant!

Many times we are afraid that the differences will be injurious to our marriage and, therefore, we try to obliterate them or pretend that they are not really there. Let us suppose, for example, that my wife and I attend a motion picture together. She enjoys the picture, its story line, and acting. But I have found it poorly directed and shallow. I can pretend that I enjoyed it for the sake of some superficial agreement. Perhaps I am intimidated by her judgment about the movie. After all, what do I know? I might not trust my own opinion of it. Or I might be trying to please her, seeking to reassure myself that we are not as different as we, in fact, are. By ignoring the differences, I may hope they will go away. Whatever the excuse, there is no reason for the pretense. If I play that game, I am doing so at the cost of some taste or preference that is important to me. In the long run, we both lose. I am denying myself by burying in silence values and opinions important to me. And I am denying my wife the chance to grow in her perception of life by seeing it through my eyes.

Similarly, when I discover that my wife is not the person I thought she was—or that I want her to be—God is inviting me to view this awareness as an invitation to growth. It is a summons with my name on it. It calls me to accommodate to the new reality of her being, and by so doing, I, myself, can become new and different. In short, I can grow.

Growth may mean grieving about what has to be given up. The developmental task to which many women are called in our culture is the risk of discovering their selfhood. This means giving up any vestige of the "clinging vine" self-image that pictures women as the weaker sex. It means that wives will dare to affirm themselves rather than live their lives through their husbands or children. Discarding the stereo-typical role of the mother-martyr, who sacrifices herself for others, often reveals to a woman her failure of nerve to live her own life.

Men, on the other hand, need to risk vulnerability and to abandon the self-image of strong warrior who feels no pain and admits no fear. In our society, men have been imprisoned in cultural expectations that make them the providers who protect God, motherhood, and country. That makes them responsible for making everyone in the family happy and taking care of everything from his wife's sexual satisfaction to the family's finances.

The marital relationship is never stable; it is always changing. Change is usually threatening, and personal growth is always painful. Yet, above it all hangs the rainbow of promise that labels the struggle "good." Facing the demanding confrontation of these changes—intriguing or threatening—we are called by marriage beyond ourselves; called out of our self contained shells; called into new being.

I have learned over the course of many married years that to love my wife means I must love her not only for the person she is, but for the person she is becoming. When love sees the other through the eyes of grace, it sees what the other person can become. My spouse is a growing, developing, ever-changing person. If I am to love her as Christ loved, then I must give up my neurotic need for her to remain as she was when I first met her. She does not exist to fulfill my needs, hopes, or dreams. Rather, I exist to help her become all that she can be, by the grace of God. To be a good mate is for me to be a good steward of her becoming.

Stewardship has to do with more than money or custodial responsibilities for planet earth. In addition to its financial and political dimensions, Christian stewardship has a relational component that a worldly spirituality calls to our attention. The divine design for marriage is not to build a bungalow where partners can settle down and live happily ever after, but to create a curriculum where they learn how to love in the grand manner of God. To grow in love, so that other people are freed from our neurotic needs—that is the intention of God in reopening the garden gate. As we learn to let go of our mates and free them from a grasping, essentially selfish, love, we are able to love them for themselves and not as extensions of our own ego.

In truth, their becoming has little to do with our needs. Consequently, marital commitment does not mean I bind my spouse to a list of expectations until death do us part. Marital commitment means I intend to share with my spouse the great adventure of kingdom living, and help her grow and become all that she can become in one lifetime—even though it occasionally hurts and ignores some of my needs. Obviously, such an understanding of love and commitment can be detrimental to the peace and comfort of marriage as many in our society think of it.

When marriage is thought of as little more than a legal contract conveying property rights, a person's individuality is sometimes crushed. Such a marriage must be characterized as an "I-It" relationship. An "I-Thou" relationship, on the other hand, respects the integrity of individual differences. Your "Thou-ness" is every bit as sacred as my "I-ness." I do not own you and have no rights over you. To honor your "Thou-ness" not only means that I will not try to mold you into my image, but that I will enable you to become all that lies within the possibility of your becoming.

Marriage is a divine calling and a holy vocation. The Bible speaks of the two becoming one flesh. That is to say, a new being is called into existence. No longer merely two separate persons doing their own "thing," but a new being that transcends and transforms the "I-ness," and the "Thou- ness," which was previously there. It is the creation of "We-ness." Within the new creation, I become a different person. My "I-ness" is not lost, denied, nor diminished. But it is transcended and transformed.

The feminist movement has sensitized our society to the rights and integrity of a woman's individuality. At least it has sensitized me about introducing Dorrine McClelland to someone as "my wife." I must allow her individuality to stand on its own merit apart from her role as my wife—one role among many in which she functions. Nevertheless, Dorrine is, in fact, my wife and I am her husband. A new reality has replaced the separateness of my "I-ness" and her "Thou-ness." Without this realization it is difficult to see why anyone would marry and choose to remain so.

Of course, not everyone is called to marriage. It does not take a marriage to produce an "I-Thou" relationship. I can deal with you as a "Thou," even as you can relate to me as an "I," each of us mutually benefiting from the encounter, growing in the relationship, respecting the integrity and delighting in the individuality of the other—all of this without being married.

I take it that the reason a couple marries is because in some way they sense, and choose to believe, that life holds greater promise in the reality of "We-ness," than in their separated "I-ness" or "Thou-ness." The reason they stay married is because they believe the new being of "We-ness" holds more promise than either the "I-ness," or "Thou-ness" existing separately.

Perhaps all of this seems rather abstract, but it is part of the experience of married people. We may not realize it at the time, and we certainly may express it differently, but when it is gone we know something devastating has happened. In the aftermath of grief over the death of his wife, C.S. Lewis tried to articulate this new being marriage had brought to him.

> The most precious gift that marriage gave me was the constant impact of something close and intimate and yet all the time unmistakably other . . . resistant . . . in a word real.[19]

It is this reality—this confrontation with the stubborn "otherness" of our mates—that calls into being the new "I-ness." The new creature that we become could never be realized or known, much less guessed at, apart from the "We-ness" of this relationship.

Marriage can call us into new being. But it can also destroy us.

The complaint, "You're not the person I married," refers to these changes in maturity taking place in our mates. It indicates that, as a partner, we are uneasy about these changes, perhaps even threatened by them. When the crisis of awareness hits, we are left with only the two choices: (1) We remain as we are and seek another partner, either inside or outside of a marriage, who seems to conform to our expectations, or (2) We do business with the new reality and enter the floodwaters of change in order to accommodate the new situation. What we believe about the God-givenness of these changes will determine whether we try to swim the tricky currents of marriage or get a divorce.

If we believe the changes taking place in our mate are a divine calling to growth, then we can assimilate the pain of change within ourselves and see it as worth the price. If, on the other hand, we like ourselves as we are—not in a self-satisfied, complacent way, but in such a way that accommodation is seen as a betrayal of God's call to be—then separation or divorce becomes the painful, but, nonetheless, equally divine calling.

It is God who has created us. The Holy One has called us into being. Our Christian vocation, therefore, is to respond to the call of Being. We must obey that calling. No one will weep at the funeral of William Robert McClelland as I will. No one can appreciate the miracle and uniqueness of my life, and the utter sadness of its passing, as well as I. Understandably, there is a certain sense of urgency about living it. We only go around once. If I do not fulfill the miracle of my being, no one can do it for me. This calling is characterized by a sense of "mustness."

People get married because in some way they believe God is creating the new being in them through the ministry of their spouses. They stay married as long as they believe marriage is a vehicle for that becoming. If experience demonstrates the belief to be unfounded, then separation or divorce may follow because persons must still follow their calling to be. Feeling that the "We-ness" is destroying the integrity of their "I-ness," some choose to end the marriage. But if the person does believe that the changes taking place in the other are God's calling to become a new creature, then the pain of change and the discomfort of growth are accepted as part of that calling. We respond obediently.

It would be nice to be able to say of everyone who enters marriage that they "all lived happily ever after," but that is only true in fairy tales and has little to do with reality or with discovery of the reconciling power of God. Unfortunately, there is no shortcut to resurrection. The journey goes by way of Calvary or it does not get off the ground.

Jesus never promised us a shortcut. "Take up your cross," he said, "and come, follow me." The cross is reality. It is the incompatibility that we experience in all of its varied forms in the real world. The Christian faith does not offer cheap grace, but it does claim that com-

137

patibility is a possibility for those who are willing to put in the hard work of making a great marriage. To couples choosing to live with the reality of disagreeable differences, the good news is that incompatibility is the norm and the labor pains of new birth hold the promise of the kingdom.

Chapter Twelve

The Risk of Loving

We were created to be lovers. We have the physical equipment for it and the emotional capacity to do it. Furthermore, we have been obliged to be lovers by no less than Jesus. In summarizing the whole of human obligation, Jesus does so with the command to love; we are to love God and our neighbor. When the apostle Paul examines all the gifts of the Spirit, he singles out love as the most important gift. "Faith, hope, love abide, these three," he says, "but the greatest of these is love" (1 Cor. 13:13). Another New Testament writer admonishes, "Beloved, let us love one another; for love is of God, and he who loves is born of God and knows God. He who does not love does not know God; for God is love" (1 John 4:7, 8). Love is a major concern of Christian spirituality.

Love also figures prominently in our culture. We see it portrayed in all of its virtue and vice on television and in the movies; we hear it extolled, lamented, and fantasized on the radio. Yet its meaning is not entirely clear. "Love" is an ambiguous term. We say to our young people, "You will know when you are in love." In fact some do, and some do not. Some think themselves in love when they are merely undressed. In a culture that easily banters the word "love" around, its meaning is unclear to many. We say with equal ease, "I love my dog," "I love your coat," "I love going to the movies," and "I love you."

The Greeks, at least, had three words in their dictionary for it. "Eros" often referred to the physical attraction between two persons. "Philia" called to mind dimensions of companionship and friendship. "Agape" spoke of unconditional love and commitment to the other. The Greeks apparently understood the complex nature of love in a way that has eluded us. Although the term "love" is used, abused, and confused, no one wants to do without it. So what does our faith have to say about it?

Although much could be said from a psychological perspective about healthy and neurotic love—who we love and why—of fundamental importance is the religious affirmation that love is of God and whenever and wherever love is present, God is present. I may not be able to love with the ability of angels, but in a world of sin—that is,

139

broken relationships—that I can love at all is a miracle of God's grace. It may be inadequate and immature love, even neurotic, self-serving, compulsive, possessive love; but to the degree that a person cares for another person and reaches out to them, it is spirit reaching for Spirit. It is of God.

It is important to establish this premise at the very beginning of any discussion of love because, although our culture worships at its altar, over the years love, along with sex, has received bad press. It has been viewed with grave suspicion.

The history of romantic love begins in France at the end of the eleventh century. Courtly love, though extolled by the troubadours, was, nevertheless, regarded by the common population as a form of insanity. The innocent-looking cherub called "Cupid" carried a dangerous weapon. His bow shot arrows tipped with poison. To be struck by one meant the loss of one's senses and infection with ecstasy.

From the church's point of view, romantic love was an offense to God because it interfered with full devotion to heavenly concerns. The twelfth century church patriarch, Peter Lombard, argued that to love one's spouse passionately was to commit adultery. Only God was deserving of such love. Vestiges of this unfortunate view still linger today. We commonly speak of "falling" in love, the same word used when speaking of "falling from grace," or "falling into sin."

But it is not just that love has received a bad press or that the skepticism concerning it trails a long history. Individual persons carry within themselves a certain fear of loving. In our technologically oriented culture, to lose control of oneself by loving another person is frightening. A young person, for example, finds it risky to say, "I love you," because the response from the beloved may be, "But I don't love you." Consequently, we hand a person a "line," trying to get a nibble— an intimation—of that person's true feelings. We reconnoiter her/his position before we risk lowering our psychic drawbridge and venturing forth. We fear rejection and rebuff, so we avoid the risk of being hurt by hiding behind defenses of pretense and manipulation. Reluctant to accept the vulnerability of love, we try to maintain control of the situation by remaining "laid back" or "cool."

Quite properly, we fear the demands that love might lay on us. There is always a fear of the unknown. What may be required of us if we give ourselves over to the requirements of love can be an awesome and unknown quantity. Bonhoeffer has reminded us that there is no cheap grace in life, and certainly none in love. Christ's crucifixion focuses for us the divine cost of love; and when our spirituality bids us love one another, that cost or demand is passed on to us. To commit ourselves to another person as the vows of marriage require "in sickness and in health, in joy and in sorrow, in plenty and in want" is to place ourselves under the demands of love. Perhaps most demanding is a love "till death do us part," which must grow and change with the other person as his or her needs change in the course of a lifetime.

The eruption of love can also be threatening. Two people make the decision to commit their lives to each other in marriage and assume, thereby, they have put behind them the possibility of ever falling in love again. Nevertheless, sometime later, they discover they have fallen in love with someone else. The discovery can be devastating. That which could not happen, should not happen, has indeed happened; and the presence of mysterious new love frightens them.

So it is very important to establish right at the very outset of our discussion that this riskiness, this demand, this threat, is of God. The Bible claims that God is love. If God is love and we are created in the image of a loving God, then a worldly spirituality calls us to risk loving, to be threatened by it, and to submit to its demands; all in the name of fulfilling our humanity. Love is that fundamental to our nature. It is elemental to the divine image in each of us. Consequently, the Bible calls us to be lovers. It prods us to develop and expand our capacity to love.

> My children, love must not be a matter of words or talk; it must be genuine, and show itself in action. This is how we may know that we belong to the realm of truth, and convince ourselves in his sight that even if our conscience condemns us, God is greater than our conscience and knows all.
>
> Dear friends, if our conscience does not condemn us, then we can approach God with confidence, and obtain from him whatever we ask, because we are keeping his commands and doing what he approves. This is his command: to give our allegiance to his Son Jesus Christ and love one another as he commanded (1 John 3:18–23, NEB).

The assertion of this writer is clear: We are commanded to love one another. His message, however, is not apt to make front-page news because, at first glance, it seems as though he is advocating apple pie, baseball, and a sound dollar.

Yet there is something strange about his message, even disturbing. He is seeking to justify such a trite invitation to love in the face of a troubled conscience. Upon closer examination, we see that he is talking about something morally risky. He is not only calling us to love in deed and in truth—that is to say, to put our action where our mouth is—he is also saying that if we do so, we could well be embarking upon dangerous waters. Loving is risky business.

Take, for example, the issue of human rights in some Third World countries. Despite our nation's outcry against the physical abuse of political protesters in El Salvador, the beatings, torture, and murder by the military death squads continue. Few official voices have been raised in objection, and Salvadoran church leaders as well as citizens who speak out against the brutality literally risk life and limb. They are called "Communists" and disappear, some never to be heard from again. Others are found brutally murdered.

Love of humanity is risky business in certain parts of the world. Examples, of course, abound closer to home, but it is always easier to make the point by looking at the speck in our neighbor's eye than examining the logjam in our own. The point, nonetheless, is: To do as John says, and put our action where our heart is, invites repercussions of the most serious sort.

But John is not only talking about loving that is physically dangerous, but referring to something that is morally dangerous as well. If we love one another, we are inviting feelings that can be threatening. I frequently conduct human awareness workshops in which participants get in touch with some of their inner feelings and have an opportunity to share them with others. Out of such sharing comes the bonding of human friendship. One of the activities involves the physical touching of other people in the group. Almost without exception, when men touch men, or participants touch someone other than their own spouses, feelings of anxiety arise. Their feelings are born of what Tillich calls "the anxiety of the possible." We are made vaguely aware of emotions that could be. We sense feelings that might develop and of which society disapproves.

Yet this is precisely what we are invited to risk if we take John's admonition to love one another seriously. We are not to hold life at arm's length nor to keep others at what might be a safe distance from us. Sam Keen once remarked that to play it cool in life is to risk becoming frigid. A worldly spirituality calls us to risk precisely these feelings and emotions that we sense as threatening and upon which society frowns.

Howard Thurman draws the conclusion that,
If all this is true, then it is clear that any structure of society, any arrangement under which human beings live, that does not provide maximum opportunities for free-flowing circulation among one another, works against social and individual health. Any attitudes, private or group, which prohibit people from coming into "across-the-board" contact with each other work against the implementation of the love ethic. So considered, segregation, prescriptions of separation, are a disease of the human spirit and the body politic. It does not matter how meaningful the tight circle of isolated

security may be, in which individuals or groups move. The very existence of such circles, whether regarded as a necessity of religious faith, political ideology, or social purity, precludes the possibility of the experience of love as a part of the necessity of man's life.[20]

Revolutionary talk indeed! The implications of loving are disturbing at best. What about national security? What about the sanctity of marriage and the unity of the family? Right away conscience is there to warn us and protect us from such subversive thinking.

It is, of course, the business of conscience to tell us to do right and avoid wrong. It reminds us that we are always to think properly and act morally. The vocabulary of conscience is laced with multitudes of "shoulds" and "oughts." As a result, conscience can be an authoritarian preacher demanding of us conduct that is correct because it is morally safe and secure. As religious pilgrims, slogging along the path of life, we can become so concerned with keeping our spiritual skirts clean that we miss seeing the scenery and the natives along the way. We are so intent on watching our step that living becomes deadly serious business. The problem with an overdeveloped conscience is that it keeps us from getting close to people.

In the eyes of the pharisees, Jesus committed the unforgivable sin by eating and drinking with sinners. For a pharisee it was far better to disassociate oneself from human beings than to be contaminated by their humanity.

Religious people, and especially those of us strongly identified with institutional religion, tend to suffer from overdeveloped consciences. Like muscle-bound weight lifters who have lost body agility and cannot move quickly, we as religious people often become conscience-bound and lose the ability to love. Like the pharisees of Jesus' day, we can become so fearful of moral contamination that we are unable to risk involving ourselves in life.

We have already noted earlier the apparent enjoyment of Jesus when the overpainted woman of the city crashed the dinner party given by Simon, the Pharisee, to wash the Master's feet with her tears (Luke 7:37–50). The Pharisee was shocked. But Jesus explained his lack of reaction by telling a story. For Simon the intended point of the story was that the gratitude of someone who has been forgiven much is obviously going to be greater than the appreciation of someone who has been forgiven a very little. The clear implication of the story was that this woman had a lot for which to be forgiven. She was certainly a sinner. No question about it. Far more of a sinner than Simon, the Pharisee, ever thought of being. Jesus, who knew full well what kind of woman she was, simply said, "Your sins are forgiven."

But she had not asked for forgiveness. She had made no remorseful confession of sins, nor done any act of contrition betraying her sense of guilt. The Pharisee was outraged because, functionally speaking, Jesus was saying, "Your sins don't matter. Your faith has saved you. Your sins have not closed you off from God because your faith—your vision of life, your sense of ultimate values, your ability to hope, your capacity to love—has saved you from hardness of heart in a way that our friend here, Simon, has not been saved. Your sins have not mattered. His relatively few sins have only served to insulate him from God. But your lifestyle has not blinded you to the miracle of grace. Live in peace."

What is conspicuously absent in this story are the words that would have made both Simon and the church feel a lot better: "Go and sin no more." But Jesus said nothing of this kind to the woman. He simply said, "Your sins have not separated you from God."

The gospels contain a similar story of a woman caught in adultery (John 8:1–11). She was dragged before the court of the Pharisees who gathered around her, ready to administer the *coup de grace*. It was an open-and-shut case. She had been caught red-handed. She deserved the death penalty because she was a sinful woman, and the law prescribed her punishment. But then this man of grace entered the scene and dispersed the crowd with the words, "Let him who is without sin among you be the first to throw a stone at her." After her would-be judges had slunk off for home, Jesus asked her, "Where are they? Has no one condemned you?" She looked up and replied in bewilderment, "No one, Lord." Jesus replied, "Neither do I condemn you."

The story probably ended there, but the church, unable to rest comfortably with such a conclusion, tacked on the words, "Go, and do not sin again." Such a demand is obviously absurd, as Jesus very well knew and his words, "Let him who is without sin . . ." make clear.

But, returning to Luke's story: Jesus did *not* condemn the woman who washed and anointed his feet, he spoke of her in a commendable way, "Your faith has saved you." We can anticipate Simon's protest, "How could a sinful woman have saving faith? What about my faith?" The Pharisee was absolutely correct in being disturbed. This is not what you would expect from a man of God! Luke has drawn us into the story and we are faced with another crisis of faith. Do we dismiss the good news because it does not fit our religious expectations, or do we accept the word on its own terms? Do we dismiss Christ as a man of God because he does not measure up to our definition of what a Savior should be, or do we set aside our preconceptions and receive the Man of Grace? What if God is not only sensuous, but scandalous as well? Do we then create a new God to worship?

The record is clear. Our God is a scandalous God. The Holy One visits this earth through the offspring of an unwed mother. God leaves the earth through the death of a man with a criminal record. The Holy Spirit reigns upon the earth in what appears to many as a drunken orgy. It is almost as if the Bible is saying you can always tell when God is around because there is the smell of scandal in the air.

So it is in this story. Sins do not matter. Blasphemy! The Pharisee concludes that Jesus is obviously not a holy man. Perhaps an imposter, but at best nothing more than a teacher—one among many, who can be taken or left alone, depending on whether or not you happen to agree with his teachings.

The sinful woman, on the other hand, sees clearly: This man is the Holy One of God. In her experience—and she has had a lot of it—she has seen both the good and the bad. She has long since given up trying to live by noble principles. Compromise has become a way of life. She is not a repentant sinner. She has not earned her forgiveness. She will be out on the streets tomorrow in the same way that she was yesterday and the day before. But she knows something. She knows that one cannot escape a sinful life. Whereas Simon lives in a fantasy world of pure right and total wrong—a fairyland in which one can escape sinfulness by a simple choice—the woman knows that all of living is tainted with sin. She is, therefore, willing to live—recklessly if necessary but, nevertheless, willing to risk living and loving.

Simon lives very carefully. He lives thinking there is an area of life that is untainted by sin and in which he can be safe. He views life as a tightrope walker, concentrating every moment on each step lest he topple off and be lost forever in the abyss. His attention is focused on his feet rather than the view. He must be very careful and cautious. His focus is riveted on what is right and what is wrong, what is good and what is bad. The Pharisee lives in a religious world of labels and distinctions, definitions and rules, all of which must be kept in mind at all times to prevent falling into "sinful" living.

The woman lives in a different kind of reality. For her life is simply a given. There are no rules that are not relative. There are no absolutes, only useful definitions that make life more or less bearable. For her, it is not a question of style, only a matter of survival.

Luke's story reminds me again of those days, years ago, when I was learning to fly. I had to practice takeoffs and landings. After one particularly awkward landing—just this side of a controlled crash—I ruefully commented to my instructor, "That was a miserable landing." His reply contained the wisdom of the ages. "It's a good landing if you can walk away from it."

In Luke's story, goodness is not some abstract concept; it is the ability to survive the landing and be amazed by life. Simon was concerned about whether or not it was a good or bad landing, a sinful or a righteous life. But the labels "good" and "bad" only make sense from his perspective. His definition of "sinful" fits only if you buy his assumption that it is important to label life and live in a maze of distinctions. As a result, the Pharisee saw Jesus, not as the Christ, but simply as a teacher, one whom you invite to your home for dinner and interesting conversation. You milk his mind for all you can get out of it. Then you say, "Wasn't that a nice evening?"

But the woman, the "sinful" woman, is amazed at something new in her life. She has encountered total goodness and sees the encounter as something fragile, something never to be encountered again, a once-in-a-lifetime event. She sees Jesus not as a teacher, but as the Precious One.

For his part, Jesus sees her as a beautiful and successful human being because she has survived. She can feel in a way that Simon cannot feel. She has survived, not nobly perhaps, nor sinlessly. But she can love. She can laugh and cry. She can give herself recklessly, touchingly, lovingly to others. She can see miracles of grace to which Simon is blind.

And there the story ends. There is no moral drawn for us. But the gospel narrative is powerful in its judgment. She is alive. Simon is dead. In his fascination with flawed living, he is in danger of missing the whole magnificent parade. It is the danger of an overdeveloped conscience.

To become the servant of the tyrant conscience is to draw the circle of life ever tighter around us in a safe and secure cocoon that, nevertheless, insulates us from the brisk winds of the Spirit.

Therefore, John reminds us that God does not command us to obey our consciences. A conscience is socially derived. It is programmed by cultural mores. We are conditioned to do right and avoid wrong as defined by cultural standards. But anthropologists point out that what is wrong in one culture may be right in another. There is no universally held right and wrong. Conscience always tells us to do what is right, but it never informs us what the right is. The point being: There is nothing particularly Christian about having a conscience, much less obeying it.

What God does require, John says, is to love one another. We are never diminished by the experience of loving. The basic affirmation we must make about love from a religious perspective, while sounding trite, is absolutely crucial to our understanding of the experience of loving: Love, whenever, and wherever it occurs, is of God—no matter what conscience says.

A second affirmation has to do with the mystery of love. It is specific. Love focuses on a particular person. We do not love everyone. We love this person or those persons, but we do not love everyone.

Maybe Jesus could love the crowds, but that is what makes him the center of the Christian faith and not you or me. He could love generally and universally, but you and I love specifically: this man or that woman.

There is always a kind of mystery about this phenomenon. To see it as a mystery seems to me a more fruitful way of looking at it than the medieval view of craziness.

Why do we fall in love with this man or that woman?

Sometimes the selection defies any rational analysis; the choice apparently is made deep in the workings of our unconscious. Sometimes the decision seems completely inappropriate and fraught with heartache. The prophet Hosea's choice of a wife, Gomer, comes to mind. She was an unrepentant prostitute who proved unfaithful time and again. While divinely inspired sermons came out of his experience, we must not forget the pain his love for her cost him.

Whenever I officiate at a wedding, I am acutely aware of the miracle that has occurred. Two specific persons—once total strangers to each other with absolutely no interest or concern in the well-being of the other—meet at a point in time. Their lives touch and they fall in love. Amazing! Mysterious! But why?

Rational explanations make as much sense as the explanation of a violin virtuoso's music: the rubbing of hair from a horse's posterior over the intestinal lining of a cat. The miracle is lost. The mystery is obscured rather than solved. Love is as unpredictable as it is grace filled. We do not decide to fall in love. It happens. As Jesus said to a dumbfounded Nicodemus, "The Spirit blows where it wills," and there is no way to predict it or to control it. The story of how two people meet, fall in love, and decide to intertwine their lives in the great adventure of marriage is, in each instance, a unique and fascinating tale.

But while we may not decide to fall in love, we do decide to marry. We commit our lives to one another in marriage because we sense the promise of "We-ness" and are dimly aware that the promise holds more fulfillment than either my "I-ness" or your "Thou-ness" does alone and separate. So we marry and the mystery deepens. Some marriages endure and some do not. Why?

As a pastor, I used to do a great deal of premarital counseling in an attempt to prepare young people for the problems and possibilities that lay ahead of them. I no longer do it. I have given up on most of it. Perhaps I would give some counseling in the basic skills of interpersonal communication, but I have come to realize that there is no way you can prepare people for the adventure of marriage. No one can blaze their path and there is no map for them to follow. Even if there were a blueprint, they are not developmentally ready to hear about it, much less read and understand it. They are in love, and their love is omnipotent. It has the power to overcome all obstacles. Love will triumph. They are in love. They are in love with each other, and that is enough. It is an exclusive relationship. It is a pure relationship. It is a naive relationship and love is all that matters.

The wisdom of more experienced lovers only gradually opens to them. Anne Morrow Lindbergh speaks of that pure relationship, typical of new lovers, in her classic, *Gift from the Sea*:

> One comes in the end to realize that there is no permanent pure-relationship and there should not be. It is not even something to be desired. The pure-relationship is limited, in space and in time. In its essence it implies exclusion. It excludes the rest of life, other relationships, other sides of personality, other responsibilities, other possibilities in the future. It excludes growth.[21]

In most cases this insight is withheld from lover's eyes for a time. Initially, they are quite content with each other. Then children come along. As parents, we find ourselves involved in nurturing and caring for the family, earning a living, and establishing identities and working out roles in the home and the community.

But after the children are gone and the nest is empty, there is time to reflect. We begin to understand that there is no permanent pure-relationship—nor should there be. There is, of course, a great conspiracy of silence about such a discovery. The church is as guilty as any in our society for nurturing, perpetuating, and enshrining marriage in the myth of the pure-relationship. But the myth is exposed by our experience. We often discover that the demand for the "We-ness" of a pure-relationship is a cover-up for selfishness. Frequently the need for "We-ness" is a failure of nerve on the part of one or both to risk living their own unique lives. Its emphasis can be at the expense of the sacredness of one spouse's "I-ness" or the other's "Thou-ness." Either or both, thereby, lose their identity.

I once visited a patient in the psychiatric ward of a hospital. She was a model mother and a devoted wife. She lived for her family and her husband. That was her problem. She was so involved with the lives of her family, she forgot to live her life. She was so caught up in their identities, she was in danger of losing her own. She so valued them, she no longer valued herself. Finally her unconscious mind rebelled. It literally threw a fit. The medical profession diagnosed it as a nervous breakdown. Whatever. It said, "Enough! It is time that you paid attention to yourself." And not until she did, did she begin to get well.

The New Testament is quite clear about what love of neighbor means. In the parable of the good Samaritan, it is clear that wherever

148

human need is seen, there will be found the neighbor in need of loving.

Unfortunately, the Bible is not as clear about what love of self means. Indeed, by the time Paul wrote his letter to the church at Rome, he was already imploring his readers not to think of themselves more highly than they ought to think (Rom. 12:3), and Luke was quoting Jesus, "If any man would come after me, let him deny himself and take up his cross daily and follow me" (Luke 9:23).

Very early in the history of the church, spirituality developed a personal piety of self-denial. Love of neighbor was understood as antithetic to love of self. Taking up our cross daily and following Jesus came to mean emptying ourselves of all personal pride, ambition, and self-worth in order to obey God's command to love and serve others. Loving others was to be done at the expense of loving ourselves. "Greater love has no man than this, that a man lay down his life for his friends," Jesus was quoted as saying (John 15:13). Early Christian spirituality, in addition to being otherworldly, developed an individual piety of self-sacrifice for the sake of others, and organized religion has been influenced by it ever since.

What is at stake theologically in this spirituality of self-sacrifice is that when we focus on the neighbor or spouse before we have fully come to appreciate ourselves, we cannot really love them. If we try to love others before we have come to realize the miracle of our own being—and are amazed by it—love of the other inevitably becomes one of two things: either an irksome duty or a copout from living our own lives. Either we love because it is an obligation laid on us by divine demand and we do it in order to score brownie points with God, or we find ourselves living our lives vicariously through others and calling it "love."

What is needed is a spirituality of self-affirmation. Unfortunately, traditional spirituality has called such affirmations "selfish" or "sinful," filling us with guilt when we do begin to love ourselves.

Further, genuine love of self is risky. It can jeopardize marriage. It endangers the other's perception of us because we are no longer willing to fit into expected roles and patterns of behavior.

In the last chapter we took note of the stresses and strains on marriage partners when they begin to discover themselves and honor those discoveries. Problems arise when this specific person whom I love and to whom I am committed begins to discover dimensions of her being, new possibilities never known to her before. Genuine love of self demands that she explore them. If I am to love this specific person, then I must come to value those discoveries and all that this birthing means for her. At its best, my spouse's "Thou-ness" becomes as important to me as my "I-ness," and more important than our "We-ness." Because of the years of trust and the story we have written together with our lives, I will see the miracle of her growth and development and value it. I will want to be what she needs for growth. I will offer myself as a trellis offers itself to the climbing rosebush. My calling as her mate, my marital stewardship of her life, means that I will free her from my neurotic needs to possess her and control her so that she may become all that she is capable of becoming. At its best, I say, that is what love looks like.

But unfortunately, and more probably, it will create in me primal fears of abandonment; and I will clutch at life and hold on to her in a vain attempt to seek security by trying to turn the clock back and keep things as they once were. As we noted in the last chapter, separation and divorce are frequently the outcome of this growth stage in a marriage. Not because people fall out of love, but because they are not flexible enough to grow and expand in love as their spouses change.

Does marriage help or hinder individual growth? It depends on your view of marriage. Psychiatrist Roger Gould offers this advice.

> As long as marriage is seen as a static arrangement between two unchanging people, any substantial change in either of those people must initially be perceived as a violation of the contract. It sets off guilt in one partner and developmental envy in the other, because it's not "supposed" to happen. Supposedly, we're to be defined by our partner's need for security and to move only when the other is ready or with his/her agreement. Such a contract makes us other defined; it distances us from self-directing impulses and adds an imprisoned quality to our life. . . . In a growth marriage, we are married and divorced many times in the sense that we are continually divorced from old arrangements and married to new ones. We negotiate from the present only—"But you were that way before" is irrelevant. No guilt about our new self surfacing. No responsibility to remain as we were. Only a responsibility to handle change with integrity and sensitivity to our partner.[22]

Marriage is like a greenhouse in which plants grow. If the plants begin to grow, and the greenhouse cannot be expanded to accommodate the larger plants, then they need to be transplanted outdoors. There is no need to blame the greenhouse for its inability to expand, nor any need to lay a guilt trip on the plants for growing. Marriages exist to nourish two people and afford them the necessary support to be the most they can be. As long as a marriage does this for the partners, the institution serves its purpose as the greenhouse serves the plants that it shelters. But if the plants outgrow the greenhouse, they are transplanted outside and no one calls it a failure or offers condolences.

Marriage is only a means to an end. To make marriage an end in itself, as the church and our society seem to have done, is idolatrous. There is no particular virtue in making a marriage survive. Some marriages should end. The purpose of marriage is not survival at any price, but to teach two specific people how to love. Because there are no two specific people alike, there are no two marriages that can ever be alike. To insist that all marriages conform to some presupposed blueprint including "till death do us part," is foolish. A spirituality that demands wedding vows be kept for a lifetime, no matter what the cost to those involved, makes marriage an end in itself rather than a means to that end. Rehearsal for kingdom living is what marriage is all about— learning the lessons of love for self and others. Maintaining a marriage at any expense when it no longer serves its intended purpose is misplaced devotion to God's will.

Make no mistake! Marriage is work, and not meant for sissies. With the divorce rate as high as it is we may suspect that many people throw in the towel too soon. But we must also recognize that in our society increasing numbers of people are getting divorces because they value themselves and their own growth more than the social expectations and pressures of maintaining their marriages. They find their marriages restrictive and suffocating. But society—and certainly the church—is right there to champion the institution of marriage and lament its breakup. In the name of supporting "basic values," it sometimes appears to be willing to sacrifice the integrity of persons. Blame is sought in one or both of the parties involved. "What a shame," we hear. "What could have been the problem?" "Who was at fault?" The result in an overwhelming sense of failure and guilt. A word of grace needs to be offered.

The good news is that life and love survive divorce. It is not the end. It is not even a failure. There is, of course, grief work to be done over losses incurred and the pain of hurts inflicted, but divorce is not a sin despite what church and society may say about it.

The scriptural prohibitions against divorce—except on the limited grounds of adultery (Matt. 5:32)—would seem to argue otherwise. When the pharisees asked Jesus if divorce was lawful (Mark 10:2-9), Jesus changed the subject by focusing on the created purpose of marriage. He took them back to the Genesis creation story. Jesus was not interested in the question of loopholes that, even Moses had said, were provided in God's law. Jesus instructed the pharisees that God had designed marriage for life, not death.

By this Jesus does not mean, "until death do us part . . ." Rather, he sees marriage as intended for life; abundant Life. Jesus sets marriage within the context of divine blessing for the world and its purpose in bringing life—shalom—to God's creation. Jesus is not interested in discussing the death of marriages. He wants to talk about life.

151

Following Jesus' line of thinking, and addressing the pharisees' concern about divorce, we could say that marriage is a scaffold used in the construction of a large, loving life. When a scaffold has done its job in building a cathedral, when it has done all it can do, it is dismantled. How foolish it would be to leave the scaffold standing as if it were important in and of itself. It is the cathedral that matters. Once the cathedral is finished, the scaffold has served its purpose and is no longer needed. It must come down. If it is not taken down, it can only get in the way of the edifice that it was intended to serve by blocking the view or obstructing the entrance. Public demonstrations decrying the dismantling of the scaffold would miss the whole point of the construction project.

When Jesus' disciples broke the Sabbath law, his defense of them is both relevant and revealing for our discussion of marriage and divorce (cf. Mark 2:27). They had been seen walking through a grainfield, threshing and eating some of the grain in their hands. They were apparently hungry, not starving to death, just in need of a little snack. The problem was the stores were closed. It was the Sabbath. In response to the pharisees' charges of sinful behavior, Jesus argued that the Sabbath is made for people, not people for the Sabbath. Clearly, the disciples had broken what the religious authorities believed to be God's law. Yet, the defense that Jesus offered, in effect, says that even the highest law, the law of God, let alone the laws of church and society, are all relative—relative to human needs. No less than the law, social institutions such as marriage are all part of the scaffold structure of a society and only exist to facilitate human growth. His defense of the disciples' actions argues that when these institutions get in the way, they are to be set aside. We are lords of the Sabbath. Not the other way around.

Which brings us to a final affirmation about love. Love is larger than marriage.

In that beautiful lyric on love in the thirteenth chapter of First Corinthians, Paul says, "Love never ends." Marriages do! If for no other reason, death ends them. But love is larger than marriage because it transcends death.

My parents had one of the truly great marriages. Its greenhouse was constantly expanding, allowing for their individual growth and development, though not without a good deal of painful work on their part. Four months after my mother died, my father also died. Shortly thereafter, I had a dream in which my mother came to me. It was typical of her for she was the one who carried on the family correspondence that kept us all in touch over the years and distance. I said to her, "It must be wonderful to have Dad back with you." "Yes," she replied, "but he's having trouble adjusting."

It was clear to me in the dream what she meant. Already she had outdistanced my father in the art of relating to others. In the four months that separated their deaths and reunion, she had grown in her ability to love others. Their marriage was no longer an exclusive relationship. My father was not the only, nor even the primary, subject of her love. My father was entering the new state of being with the old assumptions of their marriage. The problem was that those assumptions no longer applied in the kingdom of heaven.

Such an understanding of the dream is confirmed by Jesus' own words in a story told by Luke. When Jesus was asked which of seven brothers would be the husband, in the next life, of a woman all of them had married in this one, he replied, "The sons [and daughters] of this age marry and are given in marriage; but those who are accounted worthy to attain to that age and to the resurrection from the dead, neither marry nor are given in marriage . . ." (Luke 20:34, 35).

Apparently, if you have plans for marriage, now is the time to carry them out. There will be no need of them in heaven. Jesus did not marry because he had no need of a greenhouse in which to grow. His capacity to love was already kingdom size.

But that he did not marry also reminds us that marriage is not a requirement for us to become kingdom candidates. Karl Barth once observed that God could work through Russian Communism, a flute concerto, or a dead dog. There is salvation outside of marriage, which is to say, singles are not deprived of the benefits of Christ's redemptive work in the world of human relationships. The gospel claim, after all, is that God was, in Christ, "reconciling the world to himself" (2 Cor. 5:19). The world, that is! Not just that portion of it that has walked down the aisle. And, let us never forget, it was Paul—a single himself— who made the observation.

Nevertheless, marriage is a microcosm of the world, and if our faith is as the apostle Paul claims, then it must follow that in marriage the Holy One is working to bring about the new creation. While marriage is not a required sacrament of the church, it is sacramental; and it is that sacramental quality that we have explored in light of a worldly spirituality.

Marriage is given to us by God as a shalom blessing and as a means to an end. It is not the end in itself, but it does provide a preview of what the main feature playing in the kingdom is. In it, husbands and wives are served the appetizers that prepare them for the feast to come.

Sometimes we experience a bit of kingdom living in this life. Sometimes we find our capacity to love larger than our marriage. Sometimes we learn to love others—others outside of our marriages. I am not certain I know what to do with that experience. Loving is one of the risks that a worldly spirituality calls us to take. Certainly moralisms miss the significance of the experience, which continually serves to remind us that love is larger than marriage. In the last analysis, we are all part of God's family, both intended and destined to love one another as we have been loved—if not here, then hereafter.

But of one thing I am certain. It was God's idea, not ours, to create us male and female. It was God's intent, not the devil's, that we should learn to love beyond marriage. And it is a gift of grace, not a sin, when we discover that our capacity to love others has, in fact, grown beyond the innocence of the pure-relationship. The only question is whether we fight it or celebrate it. Our faith invites us to do the latter, "Beloved, let us love one another; for love is of God, and he who loves is born of God and knows God . . . for God is love."

Conclusion

In the final analysis, worldly spirituality is risky business. Like the Bible from which it is drawn, it is not "kid's stuff" and must frequently be marked, "for adults only!" We are called to risk living with a radical stewardship of wealth, called to risk living alternatives that are dangerous and sometimes seen as subversive by the power brokers of the world, and, especially, called to the subversive alternative to fear and alienation, namely, love. But it is all in the Bible.

The problem is: for many of us the Bible is like a foreign land—to borrow Robert McAfee Brown's useful analogy. We go there occasionally, but we go as tourists. And, like tourists, we feel uncomfortable and out of place. So we move on before too long and go elsewhere. As members of church and culture, we have become basically biblically illiterate. Its stories are unfamiliar to us. We are more familiar with the characters in the soaps and the punch lines of television commercials. Cut off from the roots that nourish a worldly spirituality we become, as Elton Trueblood observed, a "cut-flower generation." Separated from the earth in which our faith has been planted, we try to live on air and focus on heaven.

One of the major reasons we are so unfamiliar with the Bible is that we are too busy to read it. Busy-ness is typical of the technologically aggressive society in which we live. It is a society that brokers money, politics, and sex. Yet we try to live in such a world with our head in the clouds while our feet are mired in the mud. Small wonder, then, that we sometimes fail and fall.

Of course our faith holds out a helping hand to us, and we are lifted up to try again. We are assured of heaven. But, until we get to our journey's end, we need guidance for the path ahead. No one can make the trip for us. We must do it ourselves.

By God's grace we have come into the world. By the blessing of birth, we are required to leave behind our signatures on the pages of history, and a worldly spirituality offers us the pen.

Notes

1. John C. Banker, *Personal Finances for Ministers*. Westminster Press, 1968, p. 107.
2. Andrew Greeley, "America's World Role: Should We Feel Guilty?" Philadelphia *Inquirer*, July 18, 1974, p. 7a.
3. Dietrich Bonhoeffer, *Letters and Papers from Prison*. Fontana Books, 1960, p. 50.
4. John Claypool, *Tracks of a Fellow Struggler*. Word Books, 1982, pp. 81, 82.
5. Annie Dillard, *Pilgrim at Tinker Creek*. Bantam Books, 1974, pp. 15ff.
6. Ronald J. Sider, *Rich Christians in an Age of Hunger*. Intervarsity Press, 1978, p. 100.
7. Michael Novak, "A Closet Capitalist Confesses," *Wall Street Journal*, April 20, 1976, p. 2.
8. *Market Logic*, No. 322 (July 29, 1988), p. 4.
9. Sam Keen, *To a Dancing God*. Harper and Row, 1970, pp. 25, 26.
10. Jack Woodard, *St. Stephens and the Incarnation Church*. Washington, D.C., 1981.
11. *Life*, Vol. 66, January 24, 1969, p. 32.
12. *Life*, Vol. 53, August 3, 1962, p. 36.
13. Dietrich Bonhoeffer, *Prisoner for God*. Macmillan, 1953, p. 131.
14. D. H. Lawrence, *The First Lady Chatterly*. Dial Press, 1944, p. 52.
15. Elaine Pagels, *Adam, Eve, and the Serpent*. Random House, 1988, p. xix.
16. Edith Sommer Soderberg, *A Room Full of Roses*, rev. ed. Dramatists Play Service, 1956.
17. Derrick Sherwin Bailey, *The Mystery of Love and Marriage*, Harper, 1952, pp. 45, 46.
18. Erich Fromm, *The Anatomy of Love*, ed. Aaron M. Krich, Dell Publications, 1960, p. 206.

19. C. S. Lewis, *A Grief Observed.* Seabury Press, 1961, p. 18.
20. Howard Thurman, *Disciplines of the Spirit.* Friends United Press, 1977, p. 127.
21. Anne Morrow Lindbergh, *Gift from the Sea.* Vintage Books, 1975, pp. 73, 74.
22. Roger Gould, *Transformations.* Touchstone Books, 1978, pp. 323, 324.